A Taste of Text
An Introduction to the Talmud and Midrash

Ronald H. Isaacs

UAHC Press

New York, New York

Library of Congress Cataloging-in-Publication Data

Isaacs, Ronald H.
   A taste of text : an introduction to the Talmud and Midrash / Ronald Isaacs.
      p. cm.
   ISBN 0-8074-0857-3 (pbk. : alk. paper)
   1. Judaism—Customs and practices—Textbooks. 2. Legends, Jewish—Textbooks.
3. Ethics, Jewish—Textbooks. 4. Jewish religious education of teenagers. I. Title.

BM700.I7245 2003
296.1'2061—dc21

                                                                    2002043582

Designer: Shaul Akri
Typesetting: El Ot Ltd., Tel Aviv
This book is printed on acid-free paper.
Text copyright © 2003 by Ronald H. Isaacs
Manufactured in the United States of America
10 9 8 7 6 5 4 3 2 1

A Taste of Text

An Introduction to the Talmud and Midrash

Acknowledgments

I want to first and foremost thank my students at Temple Sholom of Bridgewater, New Jersey, for allowing me the opportunity to field test much of the material in this volume. I also want to express my deepest gratitude and appreciation to Rabbi Hara Person who allowed me the opportunity to publish this book. Her keen eye and gentle suggestions helped to clarify a number of ideas. Her wonderful insights helped to further shape the book and make it even more interesting and user-friendly.

This is my first publication with UAHC Press, a publishing house that I have always admired. I am pleased that my book will now join its many other fine publications. I am also appreciative of all the work that was put into this book by the staff of the UAHC Press, including Ken Gesser, Stuart Benick, Rick Abrams, Liane Broido, Debra Hirsch Corman, and Annie Belford Vernon.

A Taste of Text: An Introduction to the Talmud and Midrash

Table of Contents

Introduction

The Talmud

The Talmud (Hebrew for "study") is one of the central works of the Jewish people. It is the record of rabbinic teachings that spans a period of about six hundred years, beginning in the first century C.E. and continuing through the sixth and seventh centuries C.E. The rabbinic teachings of the Talmud explain in great detail how the commandments of the Torah are to be carried out. For example, the Torah teaches us that one is prohibited from working on the Sabbath. But what does that really mean? There is no detailed definition in the Torah of "work." The talmudic tractate called *Shabbat* therefore devotes an entire chapter to the meaning of work and the various categories of prohibited work.

The Talmud is made up of two separate works: the Mishnah, primarily a compilation of Jewish laws, written in Hebrew and edited sometime around 200 C.E. in the Land of Israel; and the Gemara, the rabbinic commentaries and discussions on the Mishnah, written in Hebrew and Aramaic, which emanated from Israel and Babylonia over the next three hundred years. There are two Talmuds: the *Y'rushalmi* or Jerusalem Talmud (from the Land of Israel) and the *Bavli* or Babylonian Talmud. The Babylonian Talmud, which was edited after the Jerusalem Talmud and is much more widely known, is generally considered more authoritative than the Jerusalem Talmud.

The Talmud's discussions are recorded in a consistent format. A law from the Mishnah is cited, followed by rabbinic deliberations on its meaning (i.e., the Gemara). At times, the rabbinic discussions wander far afield from the original topic. The Rabbis whose views are cited in the Mishnah are known as *Tannaim* (Aramaic for "teachers"), while the Rabbis quoted in the Gemara are known as *Amoraim* ("explainers" or "interpreters").

Thus for example, if a person wanted to find out about the laws related to Rosh HaShanah, one would go to the tractate called *Rosh HaShanah* and would find there numerous laws and customs related to the festival. Likewise, if one wanted to find the laws and customs about Shabbat, one could go to the tractate of the same name.

Rabbi Y'hudah HaNasi (Judah the Prince) is thought to be the editor of the sixty-three tractates of Mishnah in which the laws are encoded. The main editor of the Gemara is generally assumed to be Rav Ashi, who spent over fifty years collecting the material. The final revision and editing were most likely undertaken by Ravina (500 C.E.).

As the earliest rabbinic interpretation of the Bible, the Talmud is indispensable to understanding the laws and customs Jews still practice today. The talmudic discussion and its conclusions provide us with the origins of our many laws and customs. Studying the Talmud can help us search for the many important issues and values that are essential to a thinking and committed Jew.

The Midrash

Another form of rabbinic literature is midrash. The Hebrew term *midrash* ("investigation" or "drawing out") signifies study and interpretation. For the most part, the purpose of midrashic literature is to explain the biblical text from the ethical and devotional point of view. It is a way to explain internal difficulties in the text and to "draw out" meaning relevant to religious and cultural life. Midrash combines careful study of the text along with creative explanations. The word *midrash* itself comes from a Hebrew verb meaning "to inquire" and refers to a process of reading the text closely to find insights that go beyond the plain meaning of the word. There are two types of midrash. *Midrash aggadah* derive the sermonic implications from the biblical text. *Midrash halachah* derive laws from the biblical text.

The term *midrash* most often refers to the famous compilation of *Midrash Rabbah*, a compilation of the Rabbis' comments on each of the five volumes of the Torah as well as the Five *M'gillot* (Song of Songs, Ruth, Lamentations, Ecclesiastes, and Esther). Thus for example, *B'reishit Rabbah* (or Genesis Rabbah) consists of a hundred sections, each containing a chain of interpretive legends. Edited no later than the sixth century, scholars regard it as one of the earliest midrashim.

Another midrash, called *Midrash Tanchuma* (sixth century C.E.), exists in two different compilations. It derives its name from Rabbi Tanchuma bar Abba, whom it frequently quotes. It is also known as *Midrash*

Y'lamdeinu because the introductions often begin with the formula *y'lamdeinu rabbeinu* (instruct us, our master). This work contains a great deal of messianic contemplation.

The *P'sikta* comprises two separate collections: *P'sikta D'Rav Kahana* (seventh century C.E.) and *P'sikta Rabbati* (ninth century C.E.). These works revolve around the Festivals and other special occasions. The collection *Yalkut Shimoni* (thirteenth century C.E.) is a compilation from a large number of midrashic works on all the books of the Bible.

In addition to the principal midrashim listed above, there are scores of even more minor midrashim that have been assembled by Jewish scholars over the centuries.

Studying midrash can help us see beyond the text. Midrash can often assist us in making an ancient text relevant by personalizing it. And midrash offers insights on the Bible, adding new layers of understanding to elements in the text that are often overlooked.

A Taste of Text: An Introduction to the Talmud and Midrash

As Jews, we are very fortunate to be heir to an honorable system of Jewish ethics. Both the *Tanach* and rabbinic teachings and writings deal with the question of how one should behave and why. The goal of *A Taste of Text: An Introduction to the Talmud and Midrash* is to afford students an opportunity to read and study various texts that express Jewish ethical principles, culled from both the Talmud and midrash on a variety of topics. The texts are among the author's favorites and deal with sixteen different subjects. Each chapter follows an identical paradigm. First, the talmudic or midrashic text is presented, followed by a section entitled "Background of the Tale." This section provides some background material that helps to edify and make the text more understandable. The next section, entitled "What Does Judaism Say?" includes material that represents a sampling of various Jewish views related to the particular topic of that chapter. The section called "Notable Quotations" contains a variety of quotations, culled from the Bible, Talmud, midrash, and various rabbinic authorities throughout the ages. The quotations all relate in some fashion to the topic in the chapter under discussion. The final section of each chapter, entitled "Questions," provides students with questions to answer and issues to ponder or debate. To answer the questions, students will further be required to review and reread sections of the chapter, as well as on occasion do additional research.

The love of learning has always dominated our faith. It is through study of text that we learn how to lead a moral and ethical life. I hope that you will enjoy studying and getting your first taste of the texts as you begin your entrance into the vast world of both the Talmud and midrash. I would be especially grateful to learn that your study has led you to a love of learning that will continue to flourish and blossom throughout your life. Finally, I hope that this book will help to stimulate your desire to live a life that cares for the needs of other people and reflects your continuing partnership with God.

A Note about the Hebrew and Translations

Every attempt was made to find vocalized Hebrew texts for every selection. In several cases this was not possible. In one case it was not possible to locate the original Hebrew source of a text. It is hoped that despite this, the material that has been provided will serve as a basis for interesting and inspirational study.

It is also important to note that a choice was made to remain faithful to the original texts in terms of gender language. The concern with gender-neutral language is of course an issue in the modern era, but the texts date from earlier periods. They are presented here in language that reflects the original, with apology. The reader is welcome to make substitutions as necessary.

1. Jewish Healing: Visiting the Sick בִּקּוּר חוֹלִים

From the Talmud: Give Me Your Hand

Rabbi Elazar fell ill and Rabbi Yochanan went in to visit him. Rabbi Yochanan noticed that he was lying in a dark room, and Rabbi Yochanan bared his arm and light radiated from it. Thereupon he noticed that Rabbi Elazar was weeping, and Rabbi Yochanan said to him: "Why are you crying? Is it because you did not study enough Torah? Surely we learned: The one who sacrifices much and the one who sacrifices little have the same merit, provided that the heart is directed to heaven. Is it perhaps lack of sustenance? Not everybody has the privilege to enjoy two tables [of wealth and learning]. Is it perhaps because of the lack of children? This is the bone of my tenth son!" Rabbi Elazar replied to him: "I am weeping on account of this beauty that is going to rot in the earth." Rabbi Yochanan then said to him: "On that account you surely have reason to weep." And they both wept. In the meantime Rabbi Yochanan said to him: "Are your sufferings welcome to you?" Rabbi Elazar replied: "Neither they nor their reward." Rabbi Yochanan then said: "Give me your hand." He gave him his hand and he raised him.

Babylonian Talmud, *B'rachot* 5b

רַ**בִּי** אֶלְעָזָר חֲלַשׁ, עַל לְגַבֵּיהּ
רַבִּי יוֹחָנָן. חֲזָא דַּהֲוָה קָא גָּנֵי בְּבֵית
אָפֵל, גַּלְיֵיהּ לִדְרָעֵיהּ וּנְפַל נְהוֹרָא. חַזְיֵיהּ
דַּהֲוָה קָא בָּכֵי רַבִּי אֶלְעָזָר. אֲמַר לֵיהּ:
אַמַּאי קָא בָּכֵית? אִי מִשּׁוּם תּוֹרָה דְּלָא
אַפְּשְׁתְּ — שָׁנִינוּ: אֶחָד הַמַּרְבֶּה וְאֶחָד
הַמַּמְעִיט וּבִלְבַד שֶׁיְּכַוֵּין לִבּוֹ לַשָּׁמַיִם!
וְאִי מִשּׁוּם מְזוֹנֵי — לֹא כָּל אָדָם זוֹכֶה
לִשְׁתֵּי שֻׁלְחָנוֹת! וְאִי מִשּׁוּם בְּנֵי — דֵּין
גַּרְמָא דַּעֲשִׂירָאָה בִּיר. אֲמַר לֵיהּ: לְהַאי
שׁוּפְרָא דְּבָלֵי בְּעַפְרָא קָא בָּכֵינָא. אֲמַר
לֵיהּ: עַל דָּא וַדַּאי קָא בָּכֵית, וּבְכוּ
תַּרְוַיְיהוּ. אַדְהָכִי וְהָכִי, אֲמַר לֵיהּ: חֲבִיבִין
עֲלָךְ יִסּוּרִין? אֲמַר לֵיהּ: לֹא הֵן וְלֹא
שְׂכָרָן. אֲמַר לֵיהּ: הַב לִי יָדָךְ, יְהַב
לֵיהּ יְדֵיהּ וְאוֹקְמֵיהּ.

Background of the Tale

In this tale the Talmud tells of Rabbi Yochanan's empathetic visit to his student Rabbi Elazar, who has fallen ill. According to what is known about Rabbi Elazar, he was a poor man who lived in a dark room without windows. When Rabbi Yochanan enters the room to visit him, he bares his arm, from which light radiates. Rabbi Yochanan was said to be so handsome that a light radiated from his body. Rabbi Yochanan immediately notices that Rabbi Elazer is crying, and he is determined to find the cause of his pain. Rabbi Yochanan begins by ruling out several possible reasons for Rabbi Elazar's crying, including study of Torah, lack of sustenance, and lack of children.

Rabbi Elazar finally comes to the realization that he is mourning because Rabbi Yochanan, an incredibly handsome as well as warm and caring man, will someday die. Rabbi Yochanan responds, "On that account you surely have reason to weep," and the two friends cry together.

The final question Rabbi Yochanan asks concerns his desire to know whether Rabbi Elazar's suffering is welcome to him. To understand this question it is necessary to be aware of the talmudic belief that God chastises those God loves (in Hebrew, *yisurim shel ahavah*) for the sake of making them stronger and that one's suffering will eventually lead to compensatory reward. To this question Rabbi Elazar replies that he is not pleased with his suffering nor his potential reward. The story ends by Rabbi Yochanan's asking for Rabbi Elazar's hand. Rabbi Elazar complies, and he is thereby raised up. Through this interaction, some sort of healing has taken place, and Rabbi Elazar is thereby strengthened.

Jewish Healing: What Does Judaism Say?

For Jewish people, the mitzvah of *bikur cholim* (Hebrew for "visiting the sick") is an important way of serving our fellow human beings and bringing about some modicum of healing. Visiting the sick is much more than simply a social act that is to be commended. In Judaism, it is a mitzvah, a religious obligation, and is counted in the Talmud (*Shabbat* 127a) among the mitzvot to which no limit has been prescribed. In Genesis we are told that God appeared to Abraham by the terebinths of Mamre after he had just been circumcised (Genesis 18:1). According to rabbinic interpretation, God visited Abraham as he was recovering from his circumcision, and from this biblical passage the Rabbis derived the importance of visiting the sick. Just as God visited the sick, so too, we should all visit the sick and follow in God's ways. The wisdom of Rabbi Yochanan ordering his colleague to "give me your hand" has been confirmed by modern therapeutics. The touch of a person's caring hand and warm support of friendship can be a strong stimulus to well-being.

During the Middle Ages, much kindness was shown by those visiting the ill. It was quite common after the synagogue service on Sabbath morning for worshipers to pay regular visits to the sick before they returned home to partake of their meal. There was also a particular etiquette to visiting the sick. Short visits rather than lengthy ones were encouraged, and visitors were instructed not to visit when the sick person was in extreme pain.

In modern times, the religious duty to visit the sick has often become an obligation for professionals. When a person becomes ill, he or she is treated by a network of health-care facilities and medical professionals. In addition, the patient is generally visited by a clergyperson of that patient's faith, who brings comfort to patients in local hospitals and nursing facilities. Such conditions are of recent origin. For centuries, the Jewish people sought to give emotional support to those who were ill as well as to provide medical care to the extent that it was available. There were *bikur cholim* societies in Jewish communities whose function was to visit those confined by illness. Today, many synagogues and Jewish communities have their own *bikur cholim* groups, which afford members of their congregation who are ill both comfort and friendship.

Upon visiting the sick, the Jewish custom is to extend the prayerful wish that the patient be granted a complete recovery from his or her illness. The Hebrew words for a complete healing are רפואה שלמה, *r'fuah sh'leimah*. This phrase is derived from the eighth benediction of the daily *Amidah* prayer, in which the worshiper petitions God to heal all who are ill.

The *Shulchan Aruch* (Code of Jewish Law) has an entire chapter devoted to rules related to the why, when, and how of visiting the sick. All of the rules and regulations are intended to assist visitors in making their visitations more helpful to patients. The underlying ethos of the many visitation laws is the dignity of human beings and respect for their suffering. It is also quite possible that if done properly, the benefit flows not only to the person who is ill and who is given one's hand, but to the visitor as well.

Notable Quotations

1. Rabbi Acha son of Chanina said: "One who visits an invalid takes away a sixtieth of his pain." (Babylonian Talmud, *N'darim* 39b)

2. Be zealous in visiting the sick, for sympathy lightens the pain. Pray for him and depart! Do not fatigue him by staying too long, for his malady is heavy enough already. Enter cheerfully, for his heart and eyes are on those who come in. (Ethical will of Rabbi Eliezer, eleventh-century scholar)

3. Relatives and close friends visit as soon as a person becomes ill. Others should visit after the first three days of illness. (Jerusalem Talmud, *Pei-ah* 3:7)

4. We do not visit those who are ill with sickness of the stomach, the eye, the head, or any serious illness, or if it is difficult for him to speak. We do not visit him in person but we enter an anteroom, inquire if he needs anything, listen to his trouble, and pray for him. (*Shulchan Aruch, Orach Chayim* 335)

5. An enemy should not visit his enemy during his illness, for the sick person might think that his enemy rejoices in his misfortune. (*Kitzur Shulchan Aruch* [Abridged Code of Jewish Law] 193:1)

6. When Rabbi Y'hudah visited the sick, he would say: "May the Almighty have compassion upon you and the sick of Israel." Rabbi Yosei said, "May the Almighty have compassion upon you in the midst of the sick of Israel." (Babylonian Talmud, *Shabbat* 12b)

7. It was once taught: There is no measure for visiting the sick. What does "no measure" mean? Rabbi Yosef explained: "It means that the rewards for doing so are unlimited." (Babylonian Talmud, *N'darim* 39b)

8. Whoever visits a sick person helps that person to recover. Thus the purpose of visiting the sick is to cheer the patients by pleasant conversation and good advice, and by rendering them any service and inspiring them with hope. (Babylonian Talmud, *N'darim* 40a)

9. For every deficiency in the body, there is a corresponding deficiency in the soul. (Dov Baer)

10. When you visit a sick person who is without means, do not go to him with empty hands. When he awakens, be quick to offer refreshments to him and he will esteem it as though you did uphold and restore his soul. (Rabbi Eliezer of Worms)

11. Visitors must use judgment and tact when talking to the sick person, in order not to give him false hopes nor cause him despair. They should encourage him to talk about his affairs and state whether he had loaned to others or has deposited anything with others, or others with him. The sick person should be given to understand that to impart such information will not hasten his death. (*Kitzur Shulchan Aruch,* Laws of Visiting the Sick)

12. O God, who blessed our ancestors, Abraham, Isaac and Jacob; Sarah, Rebekah, Rachel and Leah, send Your blessing to _____ . Have mercy on him/her, and graciously restore his/her health and strength. Grant him/her a *r'fuah sh'leimah,* a complete recovery, along with all others who are stricken. May healing come speedily, and let us say: Amen. (*Mi Shebeirach* prayer for healing)

13. There is no affliction for which a cure does not exist. The therapy and medicine for every ill is discernible. If you seek that misfortune not befall your body, study Torah, for it is therapy for the whole body. (*Midrash Tanchuma, Yitro* 8)

14. The prayer of a sick person for his own recovery avails more than the prayer of another. (*B'reishit Rabbah* 53:14)

15. Rabbi Akiva taught: One who does not visit the sick is like a shedder of blood. (Babylonian Talmud, *N'darim* 40a)

16. One who visits the sick will be spared the punishments of the next world. (Babylonian Talmud, *N'darim* 40a)

Questions

1. Following are questions related to the story of Rabbi Yochanan and Rabbi Elazar:

    a. Why has Rabbi Yochanan come to visit?

    b. When Rabbi Yochanan asks, "Are your sufferings welcome to you?" what kind of answer could Rabbi Elazar give?

    c. Why does Rabbi Yochanan ask his friend Rabbi Elazar for his hand instead of taking it?

    d. In this story, Rabbi Yochanan tells Rabbi Elazar what has happened to him. Is this helpful to Rabbi Elazar? Why or why not?

    e. Rabbi Yochanan seems to be either wearing or carrying the bone of his son as a cherished object that is meaningful to him. What is the function of this bone for Rabbi Yochanan? Why might he show it to others? How is the bone like or unlike the photos of children that some parents carry with them in their purses and wallets?

    f. In this story the characters are both Rabbis. Does that affect the way we read and derive personal meaning from the story? If so, how?

2. Have you ever experienced illness as a "wake-up call"? Has a supportive relationship ever helped you in time of illness or suffering? Have you ever visited someone who was sick? How did it make you feel? Do you think that *bikur cholim* is an easy or hard mitzvah? Why?

3. Do you think that prayer is appropriate when visiting one who is ill? Have you ever found yourself praying with/for a sick person?

4. Why do you think that the *Shulchan Aruch* suggests that people not visit those with sickness of the stomach, eye, or head?

5. Do you think that it is appropriate to visit a sick person whom you dislike? What do you think of the reasoning of the *Shulchan Aruch* that one should refrain from visiting one's enemy because it would appear that you are rejoicing in that person's misfortune?

6. What are the best times of the day to visit the sick? Do you agree with the Jerusalem Talmud that relatives and close friends should visit as soon as they learn of the illness of their loved one, while others should wait several days?

7. What do you think are some appropriate things to bring to a person who is ill?

8. What are your personal rules regarding what to say or what not to say when visiting a sick person? Is it necessary to talk with the patient all the time one is visiting? When would "silence be golden"?

9. According to *Midrash Tanchuma,* Torah study is therapy for the whole body. What do you think this midrash means? Do you agree with its intentions? Why or why not?

10. According to the midrash (*B'reishit Rabbah* 53:14), the prayer of sick persons for their own recovery avails more than the prayer of another. Do you agree with this statement? Why or why not?

11. Why in the *Mi Shebeirach* prayer for healing do we ask for a blessing for the sick person by invoking God's relationship with our ancestors (i.e., Abraham, Isaac, Jacob, Sarah, Rebekah, Rachel, and Leah)? What does the wording of this prayer teach us about the Jewish view of God's role in healing?

2. Friendship: Acquire a Friend *(Pirkei Avot 1:6)*
חֲבֵרוּת

From the Midrash: Three Friends

There were two close friends who had been parted by war so that they lived in different kingdoms. Once one of them came to visit his friend, and because he came from the city of the king's enemy, he was imprisoned and sentenced to be executed as a spy. No amount of pleas would save him, so he begged the king for one kindness.

"Your majesty," he said, *"let me have just one month to return to my land and put my affairs in order so that my family will be cared for after my death. At the end of the month I will return to pay the penalty."*

"How can I believe you will return?" answered the king. *"What security can you offer?"*

"My friend will be my security," said the man. *"He will pay for my life with his if I do not return."*

The king called in the man's friend, and to his amazement, the friend agreed to the conditions. *On the last day of the month, the sun was setting, and the man had not yet returned. The king ordered his friend killed in his stead. As the sword was about to descend, the man returned and quickly placed the sword on his own neck. But his friend stopped him.*

"Let me die for you," he pleaded.

The king was deeply moved. He ordered the sword taken away and pardoned both of them.

"Since there is such great love and friendship between the two of you," he said, *"I entreat you to let me join you as a third."*

And from that day on they became the king's companions. And it was in this spirit that our Sages of blessed memory said, "Get yourself a companion."

Legend in *Beit Hamidrash*, Jellinek, A., ed.
(Leipzig and Vienna: Bamberger and Wahrmaan, 1938)

Background of the Tale

This legendary tale attempts to illustrate the verse in *Pirkei Avot* "Get yourself a companion" (*Pirkei Avot* 1:6). In *Pirkei Avot* the verse offers advice to the student who is eager to acquire wisdom and suggests that every student acquire both a good teacher and a suitable study partner. The tale deals with the risks that a person will take upon oneself for a close friend. In the tale a long lost friend visits another, and on arrival he is imprisoned and sentenced to die. The prisoner asks the king for one month's time to leave the kingdom in order to visit his family and put his affairs in order. He offers his friend as collateral in the event that he should not return. Surprisingly the friend agrees, and on the last day of the month the man has not yet returned. The king orders his friend killed in his stead, and as the sword is about to descend, the man returns and quickly places the sword on his own neck. But his friend stops him, asking that he die in his stead. This great act of heroism moves the king, who decides to pardon them both. Both friends become companions of the king, and it is, according to this legend, in this spirit that our Sages said: "Get yourself a companion."

Friendship: What Does Judaism Say?

"Get yourself a companion" (*Pirkei Avot* 1:6), advised Y'hoshua ben P'rachyah. Most people will tell you that there is nothing better than to have a good friend or two who can be trusted and counted upon to assist and be there for you in time of need. People often say that they have many acquaintances, but there are few who admit to having more than one or two really good friends.

One of the biblical models *par excellence* for friendship is that of David and his friend Jonathan, son of King Saul. This model of friendship is described and portrayed in the biblical Book of I Samuel. What makes their friendship especially remarkable is that each of these men had competitive interests. While Jonathan was the eldest son of King Saul and heir apparent to the throne, David, King Saul's leading soldier, was the people's choice to be the future king. Yet their potential competition never stood in the way of their abiding friendship for one another. David's greater gift of leadership only increased Jonathan's desire to be the top aide in his friend's future kingdom: "You are going to be king over Israel and I shall be second to you" (I Samuel 23:17).

The Hebrew word *chaver* is often used in rabbinic writings to mean a friend. But the word *chaver* has many other connotations as well, including colleague, comrade, associate, partner, companion, and fellow. It should therefore come as no surprise that the same Hebrew word for friend, *chaver,* is also used for members of groups that share common goals and responsibilities.

Perhaps you have heard of the Hebrew word *chavurah*. The Rabbis in the time of the Talmud were members of an association called a *chavurah*, which shared certain responsibilities and obligations. In the 1960s, a fellowship group (akin to a surrogate extended family) called the "*Chavurah* movement" began to emerge in the United States and Canada. Today, the word *chavurah* is often used to refer to a group of people who share common views and goals and who will often get together for different shared purposes. For example, a book *chavurah* will have get-togethers to discuss books in self-directed communal study.

Another Hebrew word for friend is *rei-ah*. Interestingly, the sixth of the seven wedding blessings (known as the *Sheva B'rachot*) refer to both husband and wife as *rei-im ahuvim*, which can be translated as "best friends" or "loving companions." Having a good and close friend can be extremely advantageous in alleviating some of the stresses and frustrations that are encountered in life.

Notable Quotations

1. Let the honor of your friend be as dear to you as your own. (*Pirkei Avot* 2:15)

2. Do not make friends with a person who is prone to get angry. (Proverbs 22:24)

3. On the day of your friend's success, participate in your friend's joy. (Midrash, *Kohelet Rabbah* 7)

4. One who elevates oneself at the expense of a friend's shame will have no share in the world-to-come. (Jerusalem Talmud, *Chagigah* 2:1)

5. To pull a friend out of the quagmire, do not hesitate to get dirty. (Baal Shem Tov)

6. Be first to greet your friend. Invite him to your joyful occasions, call him by complimentary names, never give away his secrets, help him when he is in trouble, overlook his shortcomings and forgive him promptly, criticize him when he has done wrong, respect him always, do not lie to him, pray for him and wish him happiness, and attend to his burial when he dies. *(M'norat HaMaor)*

7. One that harps on a matter alienates a friend. (Proverbs 17:9)

8. When you make a friend, begin by testing him, and be in no hurry to trust him. Some friends are loyal when it suits them, but desert you in time of trouble. Some friends turn into enemies and shame you by making the quarrel public. Another sits at your table but is nowhere to be found in time of trouble. When you are prosperous, he will be your second self and make free with your servants, but if you come down in the world, he will turn against you and you will not see him again.

Hold your enemies at a distance, and keep a wary eye on your friends. A faithful friend is a secure shelter; whoever finds one has found a treasure. A faithful friend is beyond price; his worth is more than money can buy. Do not desert an old friend. A new one is not worth as much. A new friend is like new wine. You do not enjoy drinking it until it has matured. (Wisdom of Ben Sira 6:7–15; 9:10)

9. Who is a leader? A person who can turn an enemy into one's friend. (*Avot D'Rabbi Natan* 23)

10. Do not judge your friend until you put yourself in his position. (*Pirkei Avot* 2:5)

11. A person should acquire a friend. One should eat with him, read with him, study with him, sleep in the same house with him, and reveal his secrets to him—the secrets of the Torah [i.e., methods of reasoning] and the secrets of worldly things. (*Avot D'Rabbi Natan* 8)

Questions

1. Of what Bible story in the Book of Genesis does the tale "Three Friends" remind you? Do you think that the allusion to the Bible story is intentional? If so, why?

2. Can you think of a story in real life where one friend was ready and prepared to sacrifice his or her life for another? Is sacrificing one's life for another reasonable, or is it taking the ethics of friendship to its extreme? Explain your answer.

3. In the tale the king is so moved by the love expressed by each friend for the other that he decides to change his verdict and pardon them both. Can you think of a time when a person in power was so moved by the acts of people that he changed his mind and modified his decision?

4. What is the moral of the "Three Friends" tale?

5. *Pirkei Avot* defines a leader as one who can turn an enemy into one's friend (*Pirkei Avot* 2:5). Do you think that this is possible? Have you ever read about or experienced such a leader?

6. *Avot D'Rabbi Natan* recommends that friends ought to eat and sleep in the same house. Is this a requirement that would still be applicable today? Why do you think it was applicable then?

7. Should friends share secrets with each other? Was there ever a time when you needed to share a secret with one of your friends?

8. Are there advantages to having friends who are Jewish? Non-Jewish? Why or why not?

9. How do you personally go about making friends? Did any of your current friendships occur accidentally, or was there a conscious effort on your or your friend's part?

10. Imagine that you and your best friend are both running for the president of your student council. Do you think that you both could do this while still remaining good friends?

11. What are some things that are sure to end a friendship?

12. Have you ever had an occasion to criticize a friend when he or she did something that you knew wasn't quite right? How did you go about your critique? How was it perceived by your friend?

13. Emerson once said: "A friend is a person with whom I may be sincere. Before him, I think aloud." What do you think is meant by this comment? How do you define a good friend?

14. Share your thoughts on some of the demands involved in preserving a lasting friendship. Have you been able to successfully fulfill these demands?

15. There is a common proverb that says: "If you want to lose a friend, lend that friend money." Do you agree or disagree?

16. Read the Book of Ruth. What are your thoughts regarding the friendship between Ruth and Naomi?

17. An important part of our personality is the general impression that we make upon each other. If our traits are found attractive by others, we may gain some friends because of these attractions. Following are traits that studies have shown to be highly desirable in attracting people to becoming friends. Share with a classmate your thoughts about each of these traits. Then talk to your classmate about other character traits that you find attractive in a person who is a likely candidate to become your friend:

Pleasantness
Standing up for one's convictions
Considerateness
Broad-mindedness
Reliability
Sense of humor
Being able to carry on a conversation

3. Hospitality הַכְנָסַת אוֹרְחִים

From the Talmud: Abraham's Hospitality

*W*hen Job's distress came upon him, he said: "Have I not fed the hungry, offered drink to the thirsty, and clothed the naked?"

God replied: "Your hospitality does not match the greatness of that of Abraham. You sat in your house and did not attend the incoming guests. You asked them regarding the food to which they were accustomed: if one usually ate wheaten bread, you gave it to him; if not, you gave him oat bread. If he was accustomed to meat and wine, you gave it to him. Otherwise, he received coarse food. Abraham, however, went outside to welcome his guests. He gave them the best bread, meat, and wine, even to those who had never enjoyed such good food. In fact, he never inquired from anyone what should be given him. He left on long tables the best viands and drinks, that whosoever wished, might come and drink and eat. "Good enough for the poor" was not the way of Abraham.

Avot D'Rabbi Natan, 7.

וּכשבא עליו ההוא פורענות
גדול אמר לפני הקב"ה רבונו של עולם
לא הייתי מאכיל רעבים ומשקה
צמאים שנאמר ואוכל פתי לבדי ולא
אכל יתום ממנה ולא הייתי מלביש
ערומים שנאמר ומגז כבשי יתחמם.
אעפ"כ א"ל הקב"ה לאיוב איוב עדיין
לא הגעת לחצי שיעור של אברהם.
אתה יושב ושוהה בתוך ביתך ואורחין
נכנסים אצלך את שדרכו לאכול פת
חטים האכלתו פת חטים את שדרכו
לאכול בשר האכלתו בשר את שדרכו
לשתות יין השקיתו יין. אבל אברהם
לא עשה כן אלא יוצא ומהדר בעולם
וכשימצא אורחין מכניסן בתוך ביתו
את שאין דרכו לאכול פת חטין
האכילהו פת חטין את שאין דרכו
לאכול בשר האכילהו בשר ואת שאין
דרכו לשתות יין השקהו יין. ולא עוד
אלא עמד ובנה פלטרין גדולים על
הדרכים והניח מאכל ומשקה וכל הבא
ונכנס אכל ושתה וברך לשמים לפיכך
נעשית לו נחת רוח.

Background of the Tale

The Book of Job deals with the problems of human suffering and records the spiritual agony of Job, a man who has tried to harmonize his experience with his belief in an all-powerful and all-loving God. In chapter 31, Job enumerates a series of virtues, affirming that he is conscious of no thought and act that he has committed to deserve such visitation of woe as has befallen him. Job claims that he has never refused to help those in need or want, nor taken advantage of the weak and unprotected.

The tale in *Avot D'Rabbi Natan* presents us with God's reply to Job's plea. God replies to Job that Job's level of hospitality does not compare in greatness to that of Abraham. The Torah describes Abraham's hospitality to strangers in Genesis 18:1–8. Here Abraham hastens to provide food for three strangers, eager to show them hospitality during the heat of the day. According to *Avot D'Rabbi Natan*, not only did Abraham provide the best food to his guests, but he went so far as to leave fine food and drink on long tables for any passerby in need of food.

Hospitality: What Does Judaism Say?

Hospitality (in Hebrew, *hachnasat orchim*) is a religious obligation, a mitzvah in Judaism. Inhospitality is viewed as ungracious behavior. Abraham, the first forefather of the Jewish people, was extolled by the Rabbis of old for his virtue of hospitality. Whenever presented with an opportunity to serve guests, he did so with swiftness and favor. After circumcising himself, Abraham is described in the Bible (Genesis 18) as moving swiftly to greet and feed his guests.

The ethical duties of hospitality occupy a very important position in the ethical teachings of the rabbinic Sages, who regard hospitality to a stranger even more highly than the reception given to the Divine Presence.

Many of the rabbinic commentators approach the prohibition of not wronging a stranger from an ethical point of view. For instance, the eleventh-century Spanish Bible commentator Ibn Ezra posits that one must not treat a stranger unjustly because one might happen to have more power than he in society and that it would not be right for one to take advantage over the stranger. Furthermore, since the Jewish people themselves were strangers in the land of Egypt, which included both political and economic insecurity, we should not tolerate exploitation. Thus, Jews are compelled to always put themselves in the place of strangers and be reminded of their vulnerability.

Rabbi Samson Raphael Hirsch, a nineteenth-century Bible commentator, posits that the care and protection of the stranger are a matter of highest ethical priority. He asserts that the surest standard by which to measure the respect for human rights and humanitarianism is to see how strangers are treated. Furthermore, the treatment of the stranger is a special test of living ethically as a Jew. As a result of our history of persecution, Jews should be more sensitive to the suffering of foreigners or strangers.

In a beautiful midrash related to Abraham, we are again reminded of the virtues of hospitality. In Genesis 21:33, we are told that Abraham planted an *eishel* (tamarisk tree) in Beersheba, and there he called on the name of the eternal everlasting God. The Rabbis interpreted the Hebrew word *eishel* as an acronym of the words representing eating, drinking, and escorting (*ochel, shtiyah,* and *levaiyah,* respectively). This suggests that the virtue of hospitality is analogous to a fruit-bearing tree, for by means of hospitality, Abraham planted a tree for himself in heaven that would produce for him fruits of reward. The Rabbis also taught that Abraham's own tent in which he dwelt had four entrances, one for each of the four directions of the world. Whoever entered one side left through a different side. In this way, a poor person seeking assistance would not suffer the embarrassment of being seen by those passing on the road.

There is some midrashic literature in which Job is portrayed as a most generous man. He is said to have built an inn at the crossroads with four doors opening in four directions, so that transients might find it easier to locate the entrance.

Perhaps the most well-known biblical statement in the Torah about the ethics of hospitality is found in Leviticus 19:33–34:

> When a stranger resides with you, you shall not wrong him. The stranger who resides with you shall be to you as one of your citizens. You shall love him as yourself, for you were strangers in the land of Egypt: "I am Adonai, your God."

Notable Quotations

1. Let your house be open wide. Treat the poor as members of your own family. (*Pirkei Avot* 1:5)

2. Rabbi Huna observed the custom of opening the door of his house when he was about to eat his meal, saying: "Anyone who is hungry may come in and eat." (Babylonian Talmud, *Taanit* 20b)

3. In Jerusalem there was a custom to display a flag in front of the door, thereby indicating that the meal was ready and that guests might come in and eat. The removal of the flag was a sign that the meal was finished and that transient guests should cease from entering. (Babylonian Talmud, *Bava Batra* 93b)

4. It is the duty of the host to be cheerful during meals and thus make his guests feel at home and comfortable at the table. (Babylonian Talmud, *Derech Eretz Zuta* 59a)

5. Ben Zoma used to say, "What does a good guest say? 'How much trouble my host goes through for me. How much meat he has offered. How much wine he has set before me. How many cakes he has brought before me. And all this trouble that he went through for me.'

"But an inconsiderate guest, what does he say? 'What trouble has my host gone through? I have eaten one piece of bread and a single piece of meat. I have had but one cup of wine. All the trouble the host has gone to has been only for his family.'" (Babylonian Talmud, *B'rachot* 58a)

6. If you go to a certain place, conduct yourself in conformity with local usage. (*Zohar* 1:144a)

7. It is unbecoming for a guest to bring another guest. More unbecoming than the two mentioned is the guest who puts his host to great trouble. (Babylonian Talmud, *Derech Eretz Zuta*, 59a)

8. Our Rabbis taught: Every scholar who feasts much in every place eventually destroys his home, widows his wife, orphans his young, forgets his learning, and becomes involved in many quarrels. (Babylonian Talmud, *P'sachim* 49a)

9. A person should not enter a house suddenly, without ringing or knocking. (Jerusalem Talmud, *Derech Eretz Rabbah* 5:2)

10. A person should not bite off one slice and return the piece into his dish. (Jerusalem Talmud, *Derech Eretz Rabbah* 9:1)

Questions

1. In order to emulate Abraham's model, *Avot D'Rabbi Natan* ordained hospitality on the part of each Jew. What were the differences between the hospitality shown by Abraham and that of Job? Can you think of modern-day comparisons of each of their models of hospitality?

2. If you were to rate your family's model of hospitality, how would it compare to Abraham? To Job?

3. What are some ways that you try to make a guest feel comfortable in your home?

4. Who is your favorite kind of guest? Why?

5. If you ate a meal in another's home as an invited guest and did not find the food appetizing, would you:
    a. praise the host/hostess
    b. say nothing
    c. tell the truth

6. Who do you feel benefits more from hospitality, the guest or the host? Who do you feel ought to benefit most? Why?

7. A guest has finished spending a day at the home of his host and leaves to return home. Can you think of some nice things that a guest could do for his host after returning home? What might a good host do for the guest?

8. There is a synagogue that requests that newcomers use blue cups at the *Oneg Shabbat* or *Kiddush* following services. The blue cup is the congregation's way of identifying a new family, enabling those in the community the opportunity to introduce themselves and make the new family feel welcome. Do you have any sort of special way in your own congregation of welcoming newcomers? Do you think this is a good thing to do? Why or why not? Would you consider your synagogue a welcoming kind of congregation? If yes, why? If not, what are your suggestions for improving it?

9. Read the following midrashic tale. What can you learn from this story about the way a host and guest ought to interact with each other?

Once Rabbi Yannai was walking along a road and he saw a well-dressed man. Thinking that the man might be a scholar, Rabbi Yannai said to him: "Would the rabbi honor me and be a guest in my home?"

The man answered: "Yes."

Rabbi Yannai took the man home and gave him food and drink. He quizzed the man in Mishnah, aggadah, and Talmud. The man was totally ignorant.

Rabbi Yannai then said: "Wash your hands and say the blessing after the meal."

The man replied, "Let Yannai say the blessing after the meal in his own house."

Rabbi Yannai then said, "Repeat after me: 'A dog has eaten from Yannai's bread.'"

The guest jumped up, grabbed Rabbi Yannai, and said: "My inheritance is with you, and you would keep it from me."

"How," asked the rabbi, "is your inheritance with me?"

*The guest answered, "Once, when passing a schoolhouse, I heard the children saying: 'Torah tzivah lanu Moshe, morashah k'hilat Yaakov [Moses commanded the Torah to us, it is the inheritance of the community of Jacob].' 'Morashah k'hilat Yannai [it is the inheritance of the community of Yannai]' it does **not** say, but rather 'k'hilat Yaakov. [Jacob's community].'"*

When the two men were reconciled, Rabbi Yannai asked, "How then are you worthy to eat at my table?"

And the guest replied, "Never have I heard an evil word spoken against me and returned to argue with the person who spoke it. Never have I seen two people arguing without making peace between them."

Rabbi Yannai then said, "You have so much derech eretz [i.e., manners], and I called you a dog!"

Midrash, *Vayikra Rabbah* 9:3

10. Jonathan and Sarah are members of their Temple's youth group. They regularly attend services on Shabbat and know the other congregants and youth group members fairly well. One Friday night they noticed an unfamiliar face among the group attending services. A woman they had never seen before was sitting alone near the back of the synagogue. A number of their friends were gathered near the front of the synagogue, waiting for the service to begin. Jonathan and Sarah exchanged puzzled glances about the presence of the stranger. They were not comfortable about ignoring her. What thoughts might be running through their minds? Why might they feel uncomfortable about doing what their friends had apparently done—ignoring the stranger? Write an ending to this anecdote: what should Jonathan and Sarah do?

11. Many synagogues now have "greeters" to welcome people as they come to synagogue for services. Does your synagogue have people who welcome guests? If so, do you like the idea? If not, do you think that assigning greeters to welcome people would work well in your synagogue?

4. Parent-Child Relationships כְּבוֹד הַמִּשְׁפָּחָה

From the Talmud: Fat Chickens

A man may feed his father fattened chickens and inherit Geihinom [hell] and another may put his father to work treading a mill and inherit the Garden of Eden.

How is it possible for a man to feed his father fattened chickens and still inherit Geihinom?

There was once a man who used to feed his father fattened chickens. Once his father said to him, "My son, where did you get these?"

He answered: "Old man, old man, shut up and eat, just as dogs shut up when they eat."

Such a man feeds his father on fattened chickens but inherits Geihinom.

How is it possible for a man to put his father to work in a mill and still inherit the Garden of Eden?

There was a man who worked in a mill. The king ordered that millers be brought to work for him. The man said to his father, "You stay here and work the mill in my place, and I will go to work for the king, for if insults come to the workers, I prefer that they fall on me and not on you. Should blows come, let them beat me and not you." Such a man puts his father to work in a mill and yet inherits the Garden of Eden.

Jerusalem Talmud, *Kiddushin* 1:7

לֵשׁ שֶׁהוּא מַאֲכִיל אֶת אָבִיו
פְּטוּמוֹת וְיוֹרֵשׁ גֵּיהִנָּם, וְיֵשׁ שֶׁהוּא כּוֹדְנוֹ
בְּרֵיחַיִם וְיוֹרֵשׁ גַּן עֵדֶן. כֵּיצַד מַאֲכִיל אֶת
אָבִיו פְּטוּמוֹת וְיוֹרֵשׁ גֵּיהִנָּם? חַד בַּר נָשׁ
הֲוָה מַיְיכֵיל לַאֲבוּי תַּרְנְגוֹלִין פְּטִימִין,
חַד זְמָן אֲמַר לֵיהּ אֲבוּי: בְּרִי, אִילֵין מְנָן
לָךְ? אֲמַר לֵיהּ: סָבָא, סָבָא, אֱכוֹל וַאֲדִישׁ,
דְּכַלְבַּיָּא אָכְלִין וּמַדַּשִּׁין. נִמְצָא מַאֲכִיל
אֶת אָבִיו פְּטוּמוֹת וְיוֹרֵשׁ גֵּיהִנָּם. כֵּיצַד
כּוֹדְנוֹ לְרֵיחַיִם וְיוֹרֵשׁ גַּן עֵדֶן? חַד בַּר
נָשׁ הֲוָה אִיטְחִין בְּרֵיחַיָּא, אֲתַת צַמּוּת
לִטְחוֹנַיָּיא. אֲמַר לֵיהּ: אַבָּא, עוֹל טְחוֹן
תַּחְתַּי, אִין מְטָת מְבַזְיָיא טָב לִי אֲנָא
וְלֹא אַתְּ, אִין מְטוֹת מִילְקֵי – טָב לִי
אֲנָא וְלֹא אַתְּ. נִמְצָא כּוֹדְנוֹ בְּרֵיחַיִם
וְיוֹרֵשׁ גַּן עֵדֶן.

23

Background of the Tale

This tale deals with the trouble and extent to which a child will go in order to honor a parent. Insulting a parent is a transgression of the highest magnitude, and in the tale we learn that one is denied entrance into heaven because of it. In the second part of the tale we have demonstrated the concern of a son for his father who may have to work for a king, infamous for his insults to the workers. Instead, the son chooses to work for the king, putting his life on the line over that of his father.

Parent-Child Relationships: What Does Judaism Say?

The Jewish people are known as the people of the book (i.e., the Bible). They are also known as the people of the family, because of the high value that is placed upon Jews to have children and raise a family that will shed honor upon them and their community. Through the many difficult and trying times during Jewish history, strong family ties and a proliferation of children have always been important strategies for Jewish survival.

The relationships within a family are very complicated. Growing up today is more complicated than it was a generation or two ago. There are often tensions today from outside forces that were less prevalent in times past. With more leisure time, there are many more organizations today competing for the attention of all family members. In addition, many families consist of two working parents, decreasing the contact time that children may have with their parents. Society is also a more transitory one, and many families find themselves making numerous moves to new communities. This can make it difficult to become acclimated to a particular community. Values and attitudes have also changed over the years, and parents and children often find their values in conflict, causing stress and tension. Both interfaith marriage and divorce have increased, each in its own way adding further challenges to family dynamics.

These days, there are a large variety of manuals and handbooks dealing with helping families through their problems. Many of these books include advice on how to better communicate with one another, on showing respect and kindness, and on caring for elderly parents.

There are numerous biblical and rabbinic passages related to the family and the home. Almost all relate to the important role of each family member, and the respect and honor that each family member is expected to show to the other. Probably the most well known of all of the mitzvot dealing with family life is the one found in the Ten Commandments that says "honor your father and mother." The Rabbis, in writing about parents' obligations toward their children in the Talmud, often talk about the importance of teaching children skills, being consistent in discipline, and never favoring one child over another.

Notable Quotations

1. There are three partners in man—the Holy Blessed One, the father, and the mother. (Babylonian Talmud, *Kiddushin* 30b)

2. Anger in a home is like worm in a fruit. (Babylonian Talmud, *Sotah* 3b)

3. A man should honor his wife and children with even more than he can afford. (Babylonian Talmud, *Chulin* 84b)

4. He who loves his wife as himself, who honors her more than himself, who rears his children in the right path, and who marries them off at the proper time, concerning him it is written: "and you shall know that your home is at peace" [Job 5:24]. (Babylonian Talmud, *Y'vamot* 62b)

5. To honor parents is more important even than to honor God. (Jerusalem Talmud, *Pei-ah* 1:1)

6. If a parent unwittingly transgresses a law of the Torah, his child shall not reprimand him saying, "Father, you have transgressed a law." Rather he should say, "Father, is that what it says in the Torah?" But in the end, aren't both expressions equally insulting? Yes. What he should really say is, "Father, the Torah says such-and-such." (Babylonian Talmud, *Sanhedrin* 81a)

7. Rabbi Tarfon's mother once walked in the courtyard on the Sabbath, and her sandal split and fell off. Rabbi Tarfon placed his two hands under her feet so that she walked on them until she reached her bed. One time Rabbi Tarfon became ill, and the Sages came to visit him. His mother said to them, "Pray for Rabbi Tarfon, my sons, for he honors me more than he should." They asked her what he did for her, and she told them what had happened. They said to her, "Even if he were to do that a thousand times, he would not have given you even half the honor demanded by the Torah." (Babylonian Talmud, *Kiddushin* 31b)

8. To what length should the duty of honoring parents go? Even were they [the parents] to take a purse of his [the child], full of gold, and cast it in his presence into the sea, he must not shame them, manifest grief in their presence, or display any anger, but accept the divine decree without dispute. (*Mishneh Torah,* Books of Judges, *Mamrim* 6:1)

9. If a child's parents become mentally ill, he should try his best to help them according to their needs until improvement is vouchsafed. If their condition becomes impossible to him, he should place them in the hands of those who can properly care for them. (*Shulchan Aruch, Yoreh Dei-ah* 240)

10. It was asked of Rabbi Ula: "How far must a child go in respecting one's parents?" Rabbi Ula replied: "Consider what a certain pagan named Dama, the son of Nathina, did in the city of Ashkelon. The sages once desired merchandise from him from which he would make a 600,000 gold *dinarim* profit. But the key to the room in which the merchandise was kept was lying under Dama's sleeping father. Dama would not trouble his father in order to complete the transaction." (Babylonian Talmud, *Kiddushin* 31b)

11. Our Rabbis taught: What is *mora* [fear] and what is *kavod* [honor]? "Fear" means that a son must neither stand in his father's place nor sit in his place, nor contradict his words, nor tip the scales against him. "Honor" means that he must give him food and drink, clothe and cover him, and lead him in and out. The Rabbis asked: "At whose expense?" Rabbi Y'hudah said: "At the son's expense." Rabbi Nachman ben Oshiah said: "At the father's expense." The Rabbis ruled that it must be at the father's expense. (Babylonian Talmud, *Kiddushin* 31b–32a)

12. Everything that your father says to you, you are obliged to obey. But if he says to you: "Let us bow down to your idols," you must not obey him, lest you become an apostate. (Midrash, *Yalkut Shimoni,* Proverbs 960)

13. The Rabbis say that the best skill that a parent can teach his child is the study of Torah, for it will provide for him in this world, and sustain him in the world-to-come. (Babylonian Talmud, *Kiddushin* 82a)

14. The parent who does not rebuke his child leads him into delinquency. (Midrash, *Sh'mot Rabbah* 1:1)

15. Rabbah said that a parent should never show favoritism among his children. (Babylonian Talmud, *Shabbat* 10b)

16. Rabbi Y'hudah said: "Anyone who does not teach his child a craft may be regarded as if he is teaching him to steal." (Babylonian Talmud, *Kiddushin* 29a)

17. If you must strike a child, strike him only with a shoelace. (Babylonian Talmud, *Bava Batra* 21a)

18. A person should not promise to give a child something and then not give it, because in that way the child learns to fabricate. (Babylonian Talmud, *Sukkah* 46b)

19. He who teaches his son is regarded as if he had taught his son, his son's son, and so on to the end of the generations. (Babylonian Talmud, *Kiddushin* 36a)

Questions

1. Read the following midrashic tale and discuss the moral of the story.

A man opened a perfume shop for his son in the marketplace that was frequented by prostitutes. The businesses in the area went their own way, the prostitutes went their way, and the young man strayed to a bad end.

His father came and, catching him with some prostitutes, began to shout, "I'll kill you, I'll kill you."

A friend who was present said to the father, "You caused your son to go astray, and now you're shouting at him. You ignored all other trades and taught him the perfume business, and you ignored all other business streets, and opened a shop for him in the middle of the prostitute area. What can you expect?"

Midrash, *Sh'mot Rabbah* 43:7

2. What do you think the Rabbis meant when they wrote, "He who teaches his son is regarded as if he had taught his son, his son's son, and so on to the end of the generations" (Babylonian Talmud, *Kiddushin* 36a)?

3. If you have a sibling(s), have you ever felt that your parents were favoring one or more of them over you? What was your course of action, and how did it get resolved?

4. In what ways is honoring parents similar to honoring God?

5. Rabbinic literature lists occasions when a parent is not responsive to a desire of a child and suggests that in certain cases a child need not listen. Examples include the choice of one's mate or asking one's child to do something that would violate Jewish law (e.g., telling a child who wants to live in Israel that he or she cannot do so). Can you think of other instances in which you believe that children have the right to choose against their parents' better wishes?

6. Another possible way to translate *mora* [fear] is "being in awe." How would you describe the difference between being in awe of a parent and honoring a parent? Would you define these the same way as defined in *Kiddushin* (see quotation 11, above)? Why or why not?

7. Imagine that one of your parents is a heavy gambler. You know that extreme gambling can be addictive. Do you feel that it is a child's obligation to try to convince his or her parent to stop gambling? Role-play a scene in which a child and parent attempt to try to discuss the issue of gambling.

8. The midrash (*B'reishit Rabbah* 84) says that a man has a greater obligation to honor his father than his grandfather. Have you ever been engaged in a conflict where your grandparents sided with you over your parents? How was the conflict resolved? Can you think of times when you have an obligation to heed the advice of a grandparent over that of your own mother or father?

9. What are some modern-day obligations that you believe parents should have to their children that were not stated in the Notable Quotations section above?

10. E. Kent Hayes, in his book *Why Good Parents Have Bad Kids* (Doubleday), defines several characteristics of good parenting, including providing structure in the home, becoming actively involved in their child's interests, working hard at communicating with their child, liking themselves and knowing how to laugh, teaching their children from an early age, and teaching their children the joy in being part of a larger community. What are your thoughts on these characteristics of good parenting? Share your thoughts on additional attributes that you believe make for good parenting.

11. Is there ever a point or a time when a child need not respect a parent? Under what circumstances? Explain your answer.

5. Repentance תְּשׁוּבָה

From the Talmud: To Pray for the Death of Another

There were criminals in Rabbi Meir's neighborhood who caused him a great deal of trouble, and Rabbi Meir prayed that they should die. His wife said to him: "What are you thinking [i.e., do you think such a prayer is permissible]? Do you justify it on the basis of the verse in Psalm 104:35: 'May sinners disappear from the earth, and the wicked be no more?' But the word that you interpret to mean 'sinners' [chot-tim] can also be read as 'sins' [chataim]; in other words, 'Let sins disappear from the earth.' Furthermore, look at the end of the verse, 'and the wicked be no more.' Once the sins will end, they will no longer be wicked men. Rather, pray that they repent, and there will be no more wicked people around." Rabbi Meir did pray for them, and the criminals did repent.

Babylonian Talmud, *B'rachot* 10a

הָנְהוּ בִּרְיוֹנֵי דְּהָווּ בְּשִׁבְבוּתֵיהּ
דְּרַבִּי מֵאִיר וְהָווּ קָא מְצַעֲרוּ לֵיהּ טוּבָא,
הֲוָה קָא בָּעֵי רַבִּי מֵאִיר רַחֲמֵי עִלָּוַיְהוּ
כִּי הֵיכִי דְּלֵימוּתוּ. אֲמַרָה לֵיהּ בְּרוּרְיָא
דְּבֵיתְהוּ: מַאי דַּעְתָּךְ? — מִשּׁוּם דִּכְתִיב:
"יִתַּמּוּ חַטָּאִים", מִי כְּתִיב 'חוֹטְאִים'?!
חַטָּאִים כְּתִיב! וְעוֹד, שְׁפֵּיל לְסֵיפֵיהּ
דִּקְרָא: "וּרְשָׁעִים עוֹד אֵינָם", כֵּיוָן דְּיִתַּמּוּ
חַטָּאִים — וּרְשָׁעִים עוֹד אֵינָם? אֶלָּא,
בָּעֵי רַחֲמֵי עִלָּוַיְהוּ דְּלַהֲדְרוּ בִּתְשׁוּבָה —
"וּרְשָׁעִים עוֹד אֵינָם". בָּעָא רַחֲמֵי עִלָּוַיְהוּ
וַהֲדַרוּ בִּתְשׁוּבָה.

Background of the Tale

The great talmudic Sage, Rabbi Meir, decides in this tale to pray for the demise and death of criminals who were causing him havoc. His wife Beruriah, noted for her knowledge of Jewish law, is astounded that her husband would think such a thought, asking him what his justification could be. She is well aware that all life is precious and that to pray for someone's death is not in keeping with Jewish thought. She proceeds to ask her husband whether he bases his decision on the verse in the Book of Psalms that says, "May sinners disappear from the earth, and the wicked be no more." She then presents two compelling reasons for changing his mind. First, she notes that the Hebrew word in the verse in Psalms, *chot-tim,* meaning "sinners," can also be read with a change in vocalization as *chataim,* meaning "sins." Using this interpretation, she explains to her husband that the verse really means that once sins disappear from the earth, there will be no more wicked people.

The tale concludes with Beruriah's suggestion to her husband, Rabbi Meir, that a better prayer with which to petition God would be that the criminals repent. Heeding his wife's advice, he prays that they repent, and his prayer is answered.

This is one of the few occasions in the Talmud when a woman reigns triumphant over a man in a religious dispute! Beruriah is famous as the only woman in talmudic literature whose views on halachic matters are seriously reckoned with by the scholars of her time. A number of women's yeshivot in the United States are named after her.

Repentance: What Does Judaism Say?

The Hebrew word for repentance is *t'shuvah*, literally meaning "to return." In Judaism it is understood that sinning is "missing the mark" and that people can get back on the right track if they choose to return to God by restoring the proper relationship of respect for God. The theme of returning was a favorite one of the Israelite prophets. For example, the prophet Hosea, speaking to his people, wrote: "Return, Israel, to your God" [Hos. 14:2]. Jeremiah the prophet warns: "Return, you backsliding Israel" [Jer. 3:12].

Repentance requires a concerted effort on the part of the transgressor to break with the past and return to better ways. Maimonides, the great medieval philosopher, devotes ten chapters to repentance. Defining perfect repentance, he offers this illustration: "When an opportunity presents itself for repeating an offense once committed, and the offender, while able to commit the offense, nevertheless refrains from doing so because he is penitent, and not out of fear or failure of vigor, this is true repentance. Even if one transgressed all his life and repented on the day of his death, all of his iniquities are pardoned" (*Mishneh Torah*, Laws of Repentance 2).

Notable Quotations

1. Rabbi Eliezer said: "Repent one day before your death." His students asked him, "How does a person know on what day he or she is going to die?"

    "All the more reason, therefore, to repent today, lest one die tomorrow. In this way, one's whole life will be spent in repentance." (Babylonian Talmud, *Shabbat* 153a)

2. In the place where a repentant sinner stands, a thoroughly righteous person is not entitled to stand. (Babylonian Talmud, *B'rachot* 34b)

3. How is one proven to be a true penitent? Rabbi Y'hudah said: "If the chance to commit the same sin arises on two occasions, and one does not yield to it." (Babylonian Talmud, *Yoma* 86b)

4. The Day of Atonement atones for sins against God, not for those against man, unless the injured party has been appeased. (*Mishnah Yoma* 8:9)

5. A twinge of conscience in a person's heart is better than all the flogging that such a person may receive. (Babylonian Talmud, *B'rachot* 7)

6. If a person repents and returns to sinning, that is no repentance. (Midrash, *P'sikta Rabbati* 44)

7. One must not say to a person who has repented [and changed his or her way of life], "Remember your former transgressions." (Babylonian Talmud, *Bava M'tzia* 58b)

Questions

1. What is the moral of the story of Rabbi Meir and his wife Beruriah? Are there ever times when one should pray for the death of another? What if you knew of a person who committed murder and was sentenced to the death penalty? Is there a prayer or some words that you might say on behalf of such a person?

2. *Pirkei Avot* 2:1 says that "when a person thinks about three things, that person will not be overcome with the desire to sin: Know what is above: a seeing eye, an ear that hears, and a book in which all your actions are recorded." Write your own modern version of things that you believe can help overcome one's desire to sin, beginning with the following line:

A person will not be overcome with the desire to sin when...

_____

_____

3. In your opinion, what is the hardest part of saying, "I am sorry?" How successful have you been in asking for forgiveness of others?

4. What is your best proof that a person is truly repentant of a mistake?

5. Read this folktale and discuss its moral.

There was once a wicked man who committed many kinds of sins. One day he asked a wise man to teach him an easy way to repent, and the latter said to him: "Stop telling lies." He went forth happily, thinking that he could easily follow the wise man's advice and still go on as before. When he decided to steal, as had been his custom, he reflected, "What will I do in case someone asks me, 'Where are you going?' If I tell the truth, 'To steal,' I shall surely be arrested. If I lie, I shall be violating the command of the wise man." In the same manner he reflected on all other sins, until he repented with a perfect repentance.

6. Rabbi Meir said that when one truly repents, the whole world is pardoned. What does this statement mean to you?

7. The Baal Shem Tov wrote that "if a man has beheld evil, he may know that it was shown to him in order that he learn his own guilt and repent, for what is shown to him is also within him." What is meant by this statement? Explain why you agree or disagree.

8. The ten days between Rosh HaShanah and Yom Kippur are known as the Ten Days of Repentance *(Aseret Y'mei T'shuvah)*. Have you ever used or known someone to use these ten days in this way? If so, describe what it was like either to do *t'shuvah* or to observe someone else doing it.

9. Maimonides wrote in his *Mishneh Torah* (Laws of Repentance 2:2) that "perfect repentance is where an opportunity presents itself to the offender for repeating the offense and he refrains from committing it because of his repentance and out of fear or physical inability." What is your definition of "perfect repentance"? Is perfect repentance possible? Why or why not?

10. Rabbi Israel Salanter once wrote that "as long as the candle is still burning, it is possible to make repairs." What does this statement mean to you?

11. Maimonides once wrote that "even if a person transgressed all of his or her life and only repented on the day of death, that person's iniquities are pardoned" (*Mishneh Torah,* Laws of Repentance 2:1). Do you agree?

6. Saving a Life פְּקוּחַ נֶפֶשׁ

From the Talmud: The Pitcher of Water

*T*wo men are traveling together *in the desert, and one of them has a pitcher of water. If both of the men drink from the pitcher, they will both die, but if only one drinks, that one can reach civilization and live. Ben Petura taught: "It is preferable that both should drink and die, rather than one of them look on while his friend dies." Rabbi Akiva came and taught: "The verse in the Torah 'that your brother may live with you' [Leviticus 25:36] means only if he can live with you must you share the water, but in cases of conflict, your life takes precedence over his life."*

Babylonian Talmud, *Bava M'tzia* 62a

שְׁנַיִם שֶׁהָיוּ מְהַלְּכִין בַּדֶּרֶךְ,
וּבְיַד אֶחָד מֵהֶן קִיתוֹן שֶׁל מַיִם, אִם
שׁוֹתִין שְׁנֵיהֶם – מֵתִים, וְאִם שׁוֹתֶה
אֶחָד מֵהֶן – מַגִּיעַ לַיִשּׁוּב. דָּרַשׁ בֶּן
פְּטוֹרָא: מוּטָב שֶׁיִּשְׁתּוּ שְׁנֵיהֶם וְיָמוּתוּ,
וְאַל יִרְאֶה אֶחָד מֵהֶם בְּמִיתָתוֹ שֶׁל
חֲבֵירוֹ. עַד שֶׁבָּא רַבִּי עֲקִיבָא וְלִימֵד:
"וְחֵי אָחִיךָ עִמָּךְ" – חַיֶּיךָ קוֹדְמִים
לְחַיֵּי חֲבֵירֶךָ.

Background of the Tale

The Talmud presents a case in which one's person's death might be attributed to the passive plotting of another. We see that the Rabbis are divided on the issue. Ben Petura chooses death for both men, rather than have one look on while his comrade dies. Rabbi Akiva uses a biblical verse to show that the life of the person in possession of the water takes precedence over that of the other person. No preference is given in the Talmud for which view is more acceptable, although Jewish law has led many rabbinic authorities to interpret the law according to Rabbi Akiva because of his prominence with regard to the law.

Saving a Life: What Does Judaism Say?

Life in Judaism is sacred, always viewed as God's gift to humankind. Deuteronomy 30:19 tells us "to choose life, so that we may live." The preservation of human life takes precedence over all the other mitzvot in Judaism. Rabbinic thinkers emphasize this principle by citing Leviticus 18:5: "You shall therefore keep my statutes, which if a man do, he shall live by them." The Rabbis add: "That he shall live by them, and not that he shall die by them" (Babylonian Talmud, *Sanhedrin* 74a).

When saving a life is involved, all Sabbath laws may be suspended in order to safeguard the health and welfare of the individual, the principle being that a life in danger takes precedence over the Sabbath.

According to Jewish law, one is not merely permitted, but required to disregard a law that conflicts with life or health. For instance, on Yom Kippur, a sick person is obliged to break his or her fast.

Jewish law goes even further, allowing its most sacred rituals to be violated where there is only potential endangerment of life. In 1848 in Vilna, a cholera epidemic broke out, and doctors advised Rabbi Israel Salanter, the leading rabbinic authority, that not only those who were ill but all should eat on the Day of Atonement, since the fast would lower the people's resistance and increase their risk of contracting the disease. Rabbi Salanter proclaimed that all the Jews should eat on Yom Kippur. He himself also joined in the eating, setting a personal example for all of his followers.

There are, however, three instances when the law takes precedence over life. If the only way one can stay alive is by committing murder, worshiping idols, or committing adultery or incest, one should be prepared to die.

In cases of idolatry and unchastity though, the specific application of the talmudic ruling is not always clear. For example, a married woman, who in the normal course of events is forbidden to have sexual relations with anyone other than her husband, is not expected to resist a rapist if doing so will endanger her life.

When it comes to murder, with the exception of self-defense, the law allows no exceptions. A person cannot save one's own life, or the life of anyone else, if it means killing an innocent person.

Notable Quotations

1. Do not stand by the blood of your neighbor. (Leviticus 19:16)

2. Adam was created alone in the world to teach that whoever destroys a single soul, the Bible imputes it to him as though such a person had destroyed the whole world. (Babylonian Talmud, *Sanhedrin* 37a)

3. The saving of life supersedes the Sabbath. (Babylonian Talmud, *Shabbat* 132a)

4. Whoever saves one life, it is as if he saved the entire world. (*Mishnah Sanhedrin* 4:5)

5. All Jews are responsible for one another. (Babylonian Talmud, *Sh'vuot* 39a)

6. The Jerusalem Talmud, *Yoma* 8:5, rules that if one stops a rabbi to ask whether it is permissible to desecrate the Sabbath and Yom Kippur in order to save a life, this delay is a form of murder. While he is busy asking the question, the patient might die. When a life is at stake, haste is required. (Rabbi Ovadiah Yosef, former Sephardic Chief Rabbi of Israel)

7. A person's lamp [soul] may be extinguished for the sake of the Holy One's lamp. (Babylonian Talmud, *Shabbat* 30a)

Questions

1. Regarding the story of the two men in the desert, one having water, what would your decision be as to who should survive?

2. What is meant by the statement in *Mishnah Sanhedrin* 4:5 that saving one life is like saving an entire world?

3. The country of France has a "Good Samaritan" law, which essentially states that if you see someone in danger and stand idly by and do not act, then you are guilty of a crime. What is your opinion of such a law?

4. What can we learn from the following talmudic story?

A man came to Rava and said to him, "The governor of my town has ordered me to kill someone, and if I refuse, he will have me killed. What shall I do?"

Rava said, "Be killed and do not kill. Do you think that your blood is redder than his? Perhaps his blood is redder than yours."

Babylonian Talmud, *P'sachim* 25b

Explain why you agree or disagree with this story.

5. What does the following story from the Jerusalem Talmud teach regarding the saving of a life?

A group of people are walking along a road when they are stopped by heathens, who say to them, "Give us one of you, and we will kill him. If not, we will kill all of you."

Let them all be killed, and let them not surrender one soul from Israel. But if the heathens single out one name, as with the case of Sheba ben Bichri, that person may be surrendered to them so that the others may be saved.

Rabbi Shimon ben Lakish said, "Only someone who is under a death sentence, the way Sheba ben Bichri was, may be turned over." But Rabbi Yochanan said, "Even someone who is not under sentence of death like Sheba ben Bichri [but anyone whose name has been specified may be turned over]."

Jerusalem Talmud, *T'rumot* 8:10

7. Kindness to Animals צַעַר בַּעֲלֵי חַיִּים

From the Talmud: Story of the Calf

Rabbi Y'hudah HaNasi observed a calf as it was being led to the slaughterhouse. The animal broke away from the herd and hid itself under Rabbi Y'hudah's clothing, crying for mercy. But Y'hudah pushed it away, saying, "Go. This is your destiny." They said in heaven, "Since he showed no compassion, we will bring suffering to him." For many years after this act, Rabbi Y'hudah suffered a series of painful illnesses. One day, Y'hudah's servant was sweeping the house. She was about to sweep away some young weasels that she found on the floor. "Leave them alone," Y'hudah said to his housekeeper. Subsequently they spoke of Y'hudah this way in heaven, "Since he has shown compassion to these rodents, we will be compassionate with him," and he was cured of his illness.

Babylonian Talmud, *Bava M'tzia* 85a

דְּהַהוּא עִגְלָא דַּהֲווּ קָא מַמְטוּ
לֵיהּ לִשְׁחִיטָה, אֲזַל תַּלְיָא לְרֵישֵׁיהּ
בְּכַנְפֵיהּ דְּרַבִּי, וְקָא בָּכֵי. אֲמַר לֵיהּ:
זִיל, לְכָךְ נוֹצַרְתָּ. אָמְרִי: הוֹאִיל וְלָא קָא
מְרַחֵם — לֵיתוּ עֲלֵיהּ יִסּוּרִין. וְעַל יְדֵי
מַעֲשֶׂה הָלְכוּ — יוֹמָא חַד הֲוָה קָא כַּנְשָׁא
אַמְתֵיהּ דְּרַבִּי בֵּיתָא, הֲוָה שַׁדְיָא בְּנֵי
כַּרְכּוּשְׁתָּא וְקָא כַּנְשָׁא לְהוּ, אֲמַר לָהּ:
שִׁבְקִינְהוּ, כְּתִיב "וְרַחֲמָיו עַל כָּל
מַעֲשָׂיו". אָמְרוּ: הוֹאִיל וּמְרַחֵם —
נְרַחֵם עֲלֵיהּ.

Background of the Tale

This tale involves Rabbi Y'hudah HaNasi, the editor of the Mishnah. The tale revolves around the theological concept called reward and punishment, a belief that one is rewarded in life by God for one's acts of kindness, and punished by God for not following in God's ways. As the tale begins, Rabbi Y'hudah HaNasi fails to fulfill the mitzvah of compassion for animals. For this transgression, he is struck down with a variety of illnesses.

Time passes, and once again Rabbi Y'hudah is presented with an opportunity for showing compassion to animals, this time some weasels. Having learned his lesson well, Rabbi Y'hudah informs his servant not to lay her hands on the animals. For this act of kindness, he is rewarded by being cured of his illness.

Kindness to Animals: What Does Judaism Say?

Judaism has always been aware of the importance of proper treatment of animals. The fourth of the Ten Commandments, which ordains the Sabbath, mandates that "the seventh day is a Sabbath to God: you shall do no work, you, your son or daughter, your male or female servant, or your cattle..." (Exodus 20:10).

In Deuteronomy 22:10, we are told that "you shall not plow with an ox and mule harnessed together." The reasoning here is that since these animals are of different size and strength, the smaller one would suffer.

One of only two mitzvot legislated in the Torah for which a reward is presented is the following: "If along the road you come upon a bird's nest with fledglings or eggs, and the mother is sitting over the fledglings or on the eggs, do not take the mother together with her young. Let the mother fly away and only then take the young, in order that you may fare well and have a long life" (Deuteronomy 22:6–7). Commenting on this law, the medieval philosopher Maimonides states that the mother is chased away to be spared the painful sight of her offspring being removed.

Maimonides's concern with the suffering of animals is also reflected in his legal code, the *Mishneh Torah:*

> If one encounters two animals, one crouching under its burden and the other unburdened because the owner needs someone to help him load, he is obligated to first unload the burdened animal because of the commandments to prevent suffering to animals.
>
> *Mishneh Torah,* Laws of Murder and Preservation of Life 13:13

The Rabbis of ancient times spoke at great length about the responsibility that humans have for animals. At a time in history when animals were undoubtedly treated very cruelly by other peoples, the Sages elaborated upon the mitzvah of *tzaar baalei chayim,* literally "compassion for the pain of living creatures."

One of the most memorable laws in all of the Talmud is one that says that ''a person is prohibited to eat until one first feeds one's animals'' (Talmud, *B'rachot* 40a). Even on Shabbat, when there are so many work restrictions, one is required to properly care for one's animals. This law was initiated when the Jewish people were primarily agriculturalists, but the law is still in force today.

The laws of keeping kosher guarantee that an animal is permitted to be eaten only if it is slaughtered in such a way as to cause instant death. All animals killed through hunting are unkosher. It is no surprise, therefore, that hunting remains a generally unpopular sport among Jews.

Notable Quotations

1. If an animal falls into a ditch on the Sabbath, place pillows and bedding under it [since it cannot be moved until the end of the Sabbath]. (Babylonian Talmud, *Shabbat* 128b)

2. No person may buy a beast, an animal, or a bird until that person has provided food for it. (Jerusalem Talmud, *Y'vamot* 15:3)

3. Jewish people must avoid plucking feathers from live geese, because it is cruel to do so. (*Shulchan Aruch, Even HaEzer* 5:14)

4. When animals lose their young, they suffer great pain. There is no difference between human pain and the pain of other living creatures. (Maimonides, *Guide for the Perplexed* 3:48)

5. Do not cook a kid in its mother's milk. (Exodus 23:19)

6. When an ox, sheep, or goat is born, it should stay with its mother for seven days. From the eighth day on, it is acceptable as an offering by fire to God. However, no animal from the herd or flock can be slaughtered on the same day with its young. (Leviticus 22:26–28)

7. In the world to come, God will punish riders who wound their horses with spurs. (*Sefer Chasidim*, paragraph 44)

8. Every creature that lives shall be yours to eat. . . . You must not, however, eat flesh with its blood in it. (Genesis 9:3–4)

Questions

1. The Torah teaches that Adam and Eve were obliged to eat of fruit- and herb-bearing plants (Genesis 1:29). There is no mention of God allowing them to eat animals. Using your imagination, write a midrash about the conversation that might have taken place between God and Adam and Eve as they learned what they could and could not eat. Read it to the class and then discuss it among your classmates.

2. How do you feel about the use of animals in medical research?

3. Do you think that animals are capable of feeling pain and emotional distress? (You may want to ask a local veterinarian for an opinion and report back to the class.) Why or why not?

4. What is your opinion about vegetarianism? Interview a vegetarian and find out his or her reasons for refraining from eating meat.

5. Why do you think that the Bible prohibits the eating of blood? What is your opinion about this prohibition? Explain your answer.

6. The Talmud (*Eiruvin* 100b) states that "if the Torah had not been given at Sinai, we could have learned modesty from the cat, honesty from the ant, chastity from the dove, and good manners from the rooster, who first coaxes and then mates." Can you explain this talmudic statement?

7. Read this story from the talmudic tractate of *Shabbat*:

> We have two opinions, the first: "If an animal has fallen into a pool of water on Shabbat, we may bring pillows and cushions to place beneath it, and if it thereby ascends to dry land, it is well and good."
>
> The second opinion states: "If an animal has fallen into a pool of water, we provide it with fodder where it is so that it should not die."
>
> The second opinion seems to say that we may provide the animal with fodder but not with pillows and cushions!
>
> There is no contradiction between the two. The second opinion refers to a case where it is possible to keep the animal alive with just fodder, while the

first refers to a case where that is not possible. If we can keep the animal alive by only feeding it on Shabbat, we should do so. Otherwise, we must bring pillows and cushions.

Babylonian Talmud, Shabbat 128b

Why not just haul the animal out of the pool? What are the two solutions here? What is the difference between them? What can this rule teach us about milking a cow on Shabbat?

8. Can you think of a time when a person will use an animal in a way that might otherwise be considered cruel?

9. In the United States, factory farming is often the method of choice for raising animals. Animals are often kept in cramped, despicable conditions. In the case of veal, the problem is extreme. In order to ensure the tenderness of their meat, factory-farmed calves are immobilized in a contraption that does not permit them to graze. Instead, they are force-fed. Do you think that Jews ought to refrain from eating any kind of meat about which it is known that the animal from which the meat is produced is treated without true concern for its welfare?

10. Read this story from the midrash and answer the following question: Why is it good to be kind to animals?

When Moses shepherded the flocks of Yitro, he kept the old sheep back because of the young ones and let these loose first to feed on the tender grass. Then he let the others loose to feed on the grass of average quality. Lastly, he let the strong ones loose to feed on the tough grass. The Holy One said, "Let the one who knows how to shepherd a flock, each according to its strength, come and lead My people." Once a kid ran away and Moses pursued it until it came to a tree where there chanced to be a pool of water. The kid stood there to drink, and when Moses overtook it he said, "I did not know you ran away because you were thirsty. You must also be tired." So he set it upon his shoulder and carried it back. The Holy One said, "Since you are merciful to the flock of a human being, you shall be the shepherd of My flock, Israel."

Midrash, Sh'mot Rabbah 2:2

11. What are some ideas and suggestions of things you and your classmates might do regarding the promotion of the welfare of animals?

8. Honesty and Truth אֱמֶת

From the Midrash: Contending Angels

*R*abbi Shimon said: When God was about to create Adam, the ministering angels split into contending groups. Some said, "Let him be created," while others said, "Let him not be created." That is why it is written, "Mercy and truth collided, righteousness and peace engaged in a clash." [Psalm 85:11]

Mercy said, "Let him be created, for he will do merciful deeds." Truth said, "Let him not be created, for he will only lie."

What did the Holy Blessed One do? He took truth and cast it to the ground.

Midrash, *B'reishit Rabbah* 8:5

א"ר סִימוֹן: בְּשָׁעָה שֶׁבָּא הקב"ה לִבְרֹאת אֶת אָדָם הָרִאשׁוֹן, נַעֲשׂוּ מַלְאֲכֵי הַשָּׁרֵת כִּיתִים כִּיתִּים, וַחֲבוּרוֹת חֲבוּרוֹת, מֵהֶם אוֹמְרִים אַל יִבָּרֵא, וּמֵהֶם אוֹמְרִים יִבָּרֵא, הה"ד חֶסֶד וֶאֱמֶת נִפְגָּשׁוּ צֶדֶק וְשָׁלוֹם נָשָׁקוּ, חֶסֶד אוֹמֵר יִבָּרֵא שֶׁהוּא גוֹמֵל חֲסָדִים, וֶאֱמֶת אוֹמֵר אַל יִבָּרֵא שֶׁכּוּלוֹ שְׁקָרִים, צֶדֶק אוֹמֵר יִבָּרֵא שֶׁהוּא עוֹשֶׂה צְדָקוֹת, שָׁלוֹם אוֹמֵר אַל יִבָּרֵא דְּכוּלֵּיהּ קְטָטָה, מֶה עָשָׂה הקב"ה נָטַל אֱמֶת וְהִשְׁלִיכָהּ לָאָרֶץ.

Background of the Tale

The midrashic tale relates an imaginary argument that God's angels have regarding whether or not it is worthwhile for God to create Adam, the first human being. The argument is given scriptural support from a verse in Psalm 85:11, which states that mercy and truth meet together, while righteousness and peace kiss each other. The implication of this verse seems to be that divine salvation is dependent upon human cooperation. When truth (i.e., righteous conduct) is practiced in the land, it receives the blessing of God's mercy.

Continuing the midrash, the angels split into groups. Some argue that it would be better for man not to be created, for man is only prone to tell lies. Others contend that man should be created because he has the potential to do kind and merciful deeds.

God, having the final word, casts Truth and its argument to the ground, thus making way for the creation of Adam, the world's first human.

Honesty and Truth: What Does Judaism Say?

From biblical times, Jewish tradition has placed great emphasis on the importance of telling the truth. The Torah says, "Keep far from falsehood" (Exodus 23:7). Moses chooses "men of truth" (Exodus 18:21) to serve as judges over the Israelites. Bearing false witness against one's neighbor is condemned in the ninth commandment of the Ten Commandments (Exodus 20:13). The Talmud puts it even more strongly when it says that "the Holy One hates a person who says one thing with his mouth and another with his heart" (Babylonian Talmud, *P'sachim* 113b).

Jewish tradition is concerned with more than the mere uttering of the truth when one speaks. One is not permitted to withhold the truth by remaining silent. To protect a criminal by maintaining silence when one can assist the law is as serious a transgression as outright lying.

People have long debated whether the fib or so-called "white lie" is a departure from truth. There is always the danger that the white lie, like petty theft, will lead in time to more serious dishonesty. But there are times when even the Jewish tradition recognizes that a white lie is permissible, especially when the interests of peace are involved. For instance, the Talmud (*Y'vamot* 65b) teaches, "Great is the cause of peace, seeing that for its sake even the Holy One modified a statement." This refers to an incident in which Sarah says that she cannot have children "with my husband so old" (Genesis 18:12). Later, God, when talking to Abraham, quotes Sarah as saying "old as I am" (Genesis 18:13). The Rabbis said that God did this in order not to give cause for quarrel between husband and wife. Thus, if a separation can be prevented, the truth may be withheld between husband and wife or between two friends, for the sake of *shalom*.

The Talmud observes several instances when telling a lie would be permissible. In *Bava M'tzia* (23b–24a) it says that "a scholar will never tell a lie except in three instances regarding 'tractate,' 'bed' and 'hospitality.'" The commentators explain "tractate" to mean that a modest scholar is permitted to declare he is unfamiliar with a tractate of the Mishnah in order not to flaunt his learning. "Bed" is understood to mean that if a person is asked intimate questions regarding his marital life, he need not answer truthfully. "Hospitality" is understood to mean that a person who has been generously treated by a host may decide not to tell the truth about his reception if he fears that as a result the host will be embarrassed by unwelcome guests.

Notable Quotations

1.   There is no salvation in falsehood. (Midrash, *Ruth Rabbah* 5:13)

2.   All lies are forbidden unless they are spoken for the sake of peace. (Midrash, *Genesis Rabbah* 8:5)

3.   Teach your tongue to say "I do not know," lest you invent something and be trapped. (Babylonian Talmud, *B'rachot* 4a)

4.   Nowadays falsehood stands erect and truth lies prostrate on the ground. (*Zohar* 2:88)

5.   The seal of God is truth. (Babylonian Talmud, *Shabbat* 55a)

6.   This is the penalty for the one who tells lies: even when such a person tells the truth, no one believes that person. (Babylonian Talmud, *Sanhedrin* 89b)

7.   People who tell lies are excluded from the presence of the *Shechinah*. (Babylonian Talmud, *Sotah* 42a)

8.   Rabbi Yosei ben Y'hudah said, "Let your 'yes' be honest and your 'no' be honest." (Babylonian Talmud, *Bava M'tzia* 49a)

9.   Where there is no truth there is no grace. (Nachman of Bratzlav)

10. A person should not promise to give a child something and then not give it, because in that way the child learns to fabricate. (Babylonian Talmud, *Sukkah* 46b)

Questions

1.   A man is told by a doctor that his sister is dying of a life-threatening disease. The patient has a maximum of one year to live. Should the truth be told to her by her brother, or should it be modified to spare her mental anguish? What values come into play in this decision?

2.   In the opening midrash of the arguing angels, why do you think God chose the advice of mercy over that of truth? What would happen now if people were judged primarily by the standard of truth?

3.   When do you find yourself most prone to lie? What effect does lying have on a person?

4.   Read this story from the Talmud (*K'tubot* 16b–17a) and answer the questions that follow:

> Our Rabbis taught: How does one dance before the bride?
>
> Beit Shammai says: A bride as she is. But Beit Hillel says: A beautiful and graceful bride.
>
> Beit Shammai said to Beit Hillel: If she were lame or blind, would you say to her "a beautiful and graceful bride," since the Torah says "keep far from a false charge" [Exodus 23:7]? Beit Hillel said to Beit Shammai: According to you, one who made a bad purchase in the market, should you praise it before him or defame it? Surely you should praise it. Therefore the Sages say: One should always be pleasant toward people.

Why does Beit Hillel rule that a person should always compliment a bride and tell her how beautiful she is, regardless of whether or not it is true? Do you agree with his ruling? Why or why not?

5.   Share with the class a time in your life when you altered the truth for the sake of peace. In retrospect, do you think you did the right thing? Why or why not?

6.   You've seen your brother take $20 from your mother's purse. At dinner your mother angrily announces that in the morning she is going to fire the cleaning lady, declaring, "She's a thief!" Your brother is silent. What would you do?

7.   The prophet Jeremiah writes that "the Eternal God is truth" (Jeremiah 10:10). What do you think "God is truth" means? In what way does falseness distance one from God?

8.   If there was a Jewish standard for advertising, how would it change the ads that people see on television?

9. Life after Death הָעוֹלָם הַבָּא

From the Midrash: Open the Gates of Righteousness

At the time of judgment in the future world everyone will be asked, "What was your occupation?" If the person answers, "I used to feed the hungry," they will say to him, "This is God's gate; you who fed the hungry may enter." "I used to give water to those who were thirsty"— they will say to him, "This is God's gate; you who gave water to those who were thirsty may enter." "I used to clothe the naked"—they will say to him, "This is God's gate; you who clothed the naked may enter"... and similarly with those who raised orphans, and who performed the mitzvah of tzedakah, and who performed acts of caring, loving-kindness.

Midrash, *T'hillim Rabbah* 118:19

עוֹלָם הַבָּא אמרו לו לאדם
מה היה מלאכתך, והוא אומר מאכיל
רעבים הייתי, והם יאמרו לו זה השער
לה׳ מאכיל רעבים הכנס בו, משקה
צמאים הייתי, והם אומרים לו זה
השער לה׳, משקה צמאים הכנס בו,
מלביש ערומים הייתי, והם אומרים לו
זה השער לה׳, מלביש ערומים הכנס בו,
וכן מגדל יתומים, וכן עושי צדקה,
וכן גומלי חסדים, ודוד אמר אני
עשיתי את כולם, יפתחו לי את כולם,
לכך נאמר פתחו לי שערי צדק אבוא
בם אודה יה:

Background of the Tale

This midrash is based on a verse in the Book of Psalms that says "open for me the gates of righteousness, that I may enter to praise God" (Psalm 118:19). Although the plain meaning of the text likely refers to the gates of the Jerusalem Temple, where it was believed that God's Presence resided, the midrash understands it in terms of the future world. Thus the gates of righteousness are understood to be the gates leading into the world-to-come. There was a rabbinic belief that when a person dies, that person will be brought before the heavenly court for judgment and asked a series of questions. The Talmud (*Shabbat* 31a) delineates the following four questions: Did you conduct your

51

business affairs with honesty? Did you set aside regular time for Torah study? Did you work at having children? Did you look forward to the world's redemption? These questions clearly demonstrate that ethics is at Judaism's core.

The midrash based on the Book of Psalms also demonstrates God's concern for how a person lives his or her life and whether a person left the world a better place for others. Such a person, deemed a righteous one, is allowed entrance into the gates of righteousness.

Life after Death: What Does Judaism Say?

Jews and Judaism have generally been much more concerned with this world than the next and have concentrated their religious efforts toward building a better world for the living. This is in marked contrast to the religious traditions of the people among whom the Jews have lived. For example, in Islam, afterlife plays a critical role, and while this may not represent mainstream Muslim thought, to this day Muslim terrorists who are sent on suicide missions are reminded that anyone who dies in a "holy war" immediately ascends to the highest place in heaven.

Belief in any type of afterlife was little pronounced in the early biblical period. During the rabbinic period, however, it began to assume a more prominent place in Jewish faith. A doctrine of the immortality of the soul developed that suggested that the body returns to the earth, dust to dust, but the soul, which is immortal, returns to God, who gave it. In addition, Rabbinic Judaism also affirmed the eventual resurrection of the body with its soul that will occur with the coming of the Messiah. (Reform Judaism rejects the idea of resurrection, and both Reform and Reconstructionist Judaism usually understand the messianic idea in more abstract metaphoric terms.) This remains an area in which each of us must confront the wonder of existence on our own and make peace on our own terms with the mystery of death.

There are a number of different ideas about the precise meaning of immortality and what form it can take. Following are several ways in which the Jewish people conceive of immortality today:

1. *Influence through family:* We live on through the life of our family and their descendants. This naturalistic view says that eternal life occurs biologically through the children that we bring into this world.

2. *Immortality through influence:* When we have influenced others to the point where they fashion themselves after us and continue to use us as a role model, this kind of eternal significance is itself a form of immortality.

3. *Influence through deeds and creative works:* Our work can outlast our life. We will continue to live on through our work and creations.

4. *Influence through memory:* People live on in the memory of those who knew them and loved them. Simply remembering people whom we admired and loved gives them eternity.

5. *Reincarnation:* Jewish mystics proposed and taught that a person's soul returns again and again in different bodies, and the way in which it conducts itself in each reincarnation determines its ascent or descent in its next visit.

6. *Resurrection:* In the past, many Jews believed that the physical body would be resurrected during the messianic era.

7. *Eternal life:* The deceased live with God and will be restored to their bodies when the Messiah appears.

8. *Rationalist view:* In contrast to the mystics, the philosopher Maimonides proposed that in as much as God is pure intelligence, our godlike qualities reside in our intellects. Therefore, in developing our intelligence and reaching for the knowledge of eternal truth, we achieve immortality.

The idea that a soul enters another living entity after the death of its body has intrigued people for centuries. It appears prominently in Hinduism, Buddhism, and the burial customs of many African tribes. While not a part of mainstream Judaism, it does have a place in the world of mystics and in Chasidim. In Hebrew, the technical term for this idea is *gilgul n'shamot,* "the turning of the souls." Mystics who embrace a belief in reincarnation posit that souls have an independent life, existing before and after the death of the body. The soul, they say, joins the body at an appropriate time, remains with it for a specified period, then takes leave of the body about the time of death, prepared to assume its next assignment in the physical world. A soul can return again and again in different bodies, and the ways in which it conducts itself in each reincarnation determines its ascent or descent in its visit.

Clearly Judaism has many different concepts of immortality. But all of these options are based on one fundamental conception: In Judaism God is just, and we are all responsible for our actions in this life. Even if a person led an uncaring life, God may still find some small deed or act of repentance that will suffice for admission to the future world.

Notable Quotations

1. Praised are You, *Adonai,* who revives the dead back to life. (*Amidah* prayer in traditional prayer book)

2. Many of those who sleep in the dusty earth shall awaken to everlasting life, others to everlasting reproach and contempt. (Daniel 12:2)

3. Better is one hour of repentance and good work in this world than all of life in the world-to-come. (*Pirkei Avot* 4:21)

4. In the world-to-come, there is neither eating nor drinking nor procreation nor business dealings nor jealousy nor hate nor competition. Rather, righteous persons sit with their crowns on their heads and enjoy the radiance of the Divine Presence. (Babylonian Talmud, *B'rachot* 17a)

5. The world is like an inn; the world-to-come, like home. (Babylonian Talmud, *Mo-eid Katan* 9b)

6. People who are just, whatever their nation, will be rewarded in the world-to-come. (Babylonian Talmud, *Sanhedrin* 105a)

7. When a person departs this world, neither silver nor gold nor precious stones accompany him. One will be remembered only for his love of Torah and good deeds. (*Pirkei Avot* 6:9)

8. The prosperity that wicked people enjoy in this world is a measure of the reward that righteous persons will receive in the world-to-come. (*Midrash Psalm* 37:3)

9. There is a place in Eden and in *Geihinom* for every soul. The righteous receives his place and the place of a wicked man as well. By the same token, the wicked man receives his own place and the place of the righteous person. (Babylonian Talmud, *Chagigah* 15a)

10. No person partakes of the enjoyment of the world-to-come because of his father's merits. (*Midrash Psalm* 146:2)

11. In paradise there are seven sections for the various types of pious souls, and a separate division of seven sections for the souls of pious women. (Babylonian Talmud, *Chagigah* 12b)

12. Rabbi Yochanan claimed that a partition of only a handbreadth, the width of four inches, separates hell and heaven. (Midrash, *Kohelet Rabbah* 7)

13. Rabbi Shimon ben Lakish said: "In the future that is to be, there will be no *Geihinom*. But God will take the sun out of its orbit, and in its heat the righteous will be healed and the wicked consumed." (Babylonian Talmud, *N'darim* 8b)

14. The wise ones find rest neither in this world nor in the world-to-come, but "they shall ascend from strength to strength until they appear before God in Zion" [Psalm 84:8]. (Talmud, *B'rachot* 64a)

15. Rabbi Shimon ben Elazar said that in this world the wicked are not punished until the righteous are rewarded, for in the next world "his breath goes forth, he returns to the dust" [Psalm 146:4]. (*Avot D'Rabbi Natan* 32)

16. Rabbi Yochanan said: "All our prophets foretell only what will happen in the days of the Messiah, in the ideal future state here on earth. As for the world beyond the grave, no eye has seen, and no ear has heard, but God alone knows what He has prepared for those who wait for Him." (Babylonian Talmud, *B'rachot* 34b)

17. In the time to come, the impulse to evil will have no power. (Midrash, *B'reishit Rabbah* 48:11)

18. Queen Cleopatra asked Rabbi Meir: I know the dead will come back to life. But when they rise up, will they arise nude or clad in their garments? Rabbi Meir replied: You may come to the answer by inference from a grain of wheat. If a grain of wheat, which is buried naked, sprouts forth clad in many robes, how much more so the righteous, who are buried in their clothing. (Babylonian Talmud, *Sanhedrin* 90b)

19. In the school of Elijah it was taught: The righteous whom the Holy One will quicken will not return to the dust. You may ask, "In the thousand years during which the Holy One will renew His world, what will they do?" The Holy One will provide them with wings like eagles, and they will fly above the water. (Babylonian Talmud, *Sanhedrin* 92a–b)

20. Rabbi Elazar HaKappar taught: "They that are born are destined to die. And the dead are destined to be brought to life again. The living [i.e, the resurrected] are destined after death to be judged." (*Pirkei Avot* 4:28)

Questions

1. Of the various conceptions of the afterlife presented in this chapter, which comes closest to your own personal belief?

2. What is your understanding of the blessing in the *Amidah* that praises God for reviving the dead? The editors of the Reform prayer book changed this line to "source of all life." Why do you think they made this change? What are the different implications of each version?

3. What do you think is meant by the talmudic statement in *Mo-eid Katan* 9b that "the world is like an inn; the world-to-come, like home"?

4. If you believe in a future world, what is your conception of it?

5. The conclusion of the *El Malei Rachamim* prayer recited at funerals and *Yizkor* memorial services ends with the words "may _____ rest eternally in peace." What does this phrase mean to you?

6. What is your understanding of a person's soul? How would you define it?

7. Proverbs 20:27 says that "the soul is God's candle." What does this mean to you?

8. The Talmud (*Sanhedrin* 90a) says that "whoever has a law mentioned in his name in this world, his lips whisper in the grave." What does this mean to you?

9. What is your personal understanding of reward and punishment in the world-to-come?

10. Care of the Body שְׁמִירַת הַגּוּף

From the Midrash: Hillel and the Bathhouse

The story is told of Hillel that when he had finished a lesson with his students, he accompanied them part of the way. They said to him, "Master, where are you going?" He answered, "To perform a religious duty." They asked, "Which religious duty?" He answered, "To bathe in the bathhouse." They questioned, "Is that a religious duty?" He answered them, "If somebody is appointed to scrape and clean the statues of the king that are set up in the theaters and circuses, and is paid to do the work, and furthermore associates with the nobility, how much more so should I, who am created in the divine image and likeness, take care of my body?"

Midrash, *Vayikra Rabbah* 34:3

לֶה הִלֵּל הַזָּקֵן שֶׁבְּשָׁעָה שֶׁהָיָה
נִפְטָר מִתַּלְמִידָיו הָיָה מְהַלֵּךְ וְהוֹלֵךְ
עִמָּם. אָמְרוּ לוֹ תַּלְמִידָיו: רַבִּי לְהֵיכָן
אַתָּה הוֹלֵךְ? אָמַר לָהֶם לַעֲשׂוֹת מִצְוָה.
אָמְרוּ לוֹ: וְכִי מַה מִּצְוָה זוֹ? אָמַר לָהֶן:
לִרְחֹץ בְּבֵית הַמֶּרְחָץ אָמְרוּ לוֹ: וְכִי זוֹ
מִצְוָה הִיא? אָמַר לָהֶם: הֵן, מָה אִם
אִיקוֹנִין שֶׁל מְלָכִים שֶׁמַּעֲמִידִים אוֹתוֹ
בְּבָתֵּי טַרְטִיאוֹת וּבְבָתֵּי קִרְקָסִיאוֹת מִי
שֶׁנִּתְמַנָּה עֲלֵיהֶם הוּא מוֹרְקָן וְשׁוֹטְפָן
וְהֵן מַעֲלִין לוֹ מְזוֹנוֹת וְלֹא עוֹד אֶלָּא
שֶׁהוּא מִתְגַּדֵּל עִם גְּדוֹלֵי מַלְכוּת אֲנִי
שֶׁנִּבְרֵאתִי בְּצֶלֶם וּבִדְמוּת, דִּכְתִיב: כִּי
בְּצֶלֶם אֱלֹהִים עָשָׂה אֶת הָאָדָם עאכ"ו.

Background of the Tale

This rabbinic tale reflects a basic Jewish teaching, respect and care for the body. In the course of his conversation, Hillel makes the point to his students that not only must a person be concerned about knowledge and intellect, but one must also be concerned about the care of the body. He compares the way a person hired to take care of the statues of the king (in addition to being paid) is honored by being allowed to associate with the nobility of the community to the fact that God has created our bodies and we have, therefore, so much more of an obligation to care for them. We are not directly paid, but since we have a religious obligation to care for the body that was created in God's image, we are allowed to associate with the King Himself.

Care of the Body: What Does Judaism Say?

Human beings are created in the image of God, thus possessing dignity and value. Rabbinic authorities have always viewed the body as being imbued with sanctity. It is a gift from God, who lends it to us for the duration of our lives and reclaims it only upon our death.

Because of the underlying rabbinic principle that our bodies belong to God, many responsibilities related to the body emerge. First, we must take reasonable care of our bodies. Such obligations include proper hygiene (including bathing and wearing clean clothes), sleep, exercise, and proper diet. Neglecting the body or abusing it is a transgression that profanes the very name of God.

In addition, the rabbinic authorities obligate us to avoid endangering our health. That is why Jewish law, for example, forbids a sick person from fasting on Yom Kippur. Such a fast, it is reasoned, might cause further injury to one who is ill. In addition, it is the duty of a physician to heal the sick, and it is the religious duty of Jews to seek out professional medical attention when needed.

The Jewish mode for attaining holiness is to use all of one's bodily energies to perform God's commandments. Even bodily pleasures are positively commanded, including eating three festive meals in celebration of the holy Sabbath, bathing and wearing festive clothing in honor of the day, and enjoying the pleasures that come with lovemaking and propagation.

Bodily pleasures are best enjoyed when they have the specific goal of enhancing one's ability to do God's will and thus helping one to live a life of holiness. In the words of Maimonides:

> One who regulates one's life in accordance with the laws of medicine with the sole motive of maintaining a sound and vigorous physique and begetting children to do his work and labor for his benefit is not following the right course. A person should aim to maintain physical health and vigor in order that his soul may be upright, in a condition to know God. Whoever throughout his life follows this course will be continually serving God, even while engaged in business and even during cohabitation, because his purpose in all that he does will be to satisfy his needs in order to have a sound body with which to serve God. Even when he sleeps and seeks repose to calm his mind and rest his body so as not to fall sick and be incapacitated from serving God, his sleep is service of the Almighty.
>
> *Mishneh Torah*, Laws of Ethics 3:3

The *Kitzur Shulchan Aruch* (Abridged Code of Jewish Law) best sums up the rabbinic attitude toward caring for the body in these two passages:

Since it is the will of the Almighty that man's body be kept healthy and strong, because it is impossible for a man to have knowledge of his Creator when ill, it is therefore his duty to shun anything that may waste his body and to strive to acquire habits that will help him to become healthy. Thus it is written [Deuteronomy 4:15]: "Take you, therefore, good heed of your souls."

Kitzur Shulchan Aruch 32

Our rabbis, of blessed memory, said (Babylonian Talmud, *B'rachot* 63a): "Which is a short verse upon which all the principles of Torah depend? It is Proverbs 3:6: 'In all ways we must acknowledge God.' This means that in all of our actions, even those we do in order to sustain life, we must acknowledge God and do them for the sake of God's name, blessed be the One. For instance, eating, drinking, walking, sitting, lying down, rising, having sexual intercourse, talking—all acts to sustain life should be done for the sake of worshiping our Creator or doing something that will be conducive to the service of God."

Kitzur Shulchan Aruch 31

Notable Quotations

1. Samuel said: "Sleep at the break of dawn is as important as tempering is for iron." (Babylonian Talmud, *B'rachot* 62b)

2. It is forbidden to live in a city that does not have a vegetable garden. (Jerusalem Talmud, *Kiddushin* 4:12, 66d)

3. Rav said to his son Chiya: "Don't fall into the habit of taking drugs, don't leap over a sewer, don't have your teeth pulled, and don't provoke serpents." (Babylonian Talmud, *P'sachim* 113a)

4. Clothes worn during the day should not be worn at night. (Babylonian Talmud, *M'nachot* 43)

5. Coins should not be placed in the mouth because they may have been touched by persons suffering from contagious diseases. (Maimonides, *Mishneh Torah, Rotzei-ach* 12:4)

6. Rinse your cup before and after drinking it. (Babylonian Talmud, *Tamid* 27b)

7. Those who eat food with unwashed hands endanger their health, because they are full of dangerous germs. (Babylonian Talmud, *Yoma* 77b)

8. One who denies oneself proper food is considered a transgressor. (Babylonian Talmud, *Taanit* 11a)

9. A properly balanced diet, avoidance of overeating, and attention to the calls of nature on time prevent intestinal trouble. (Babylonian Talmud, *Gittin* 70a)

10. Exercise removes the harm caused by most bad habits, which most people have. Violent exercise causes fatigue, and not everyone can stand fatigue, or needs it. (Maimonides, *The Preservation of Youth*)

11. The body is the soul's house. (Philo Judaeus)

Questions

1. Read the following prayer, *Asher Yatzar,* which appears in the early part of the daily *Shacharit* (morning) worship service. On what occasions in your life might you choose to recite this prayer? What experience do you think caused the writer to compose the prayer in the first place?

> Blessed is our Eternal God, Creator of the universe, who has made our bodies with wisdom, combining veins, arteries, and vital organs into a finely balanced network. Wondrous Fashioner and Sustainer of life, Source of our health and our strength, we give You thanks and praise.
>
> Translation, *Gates of Prayer*

2. List any prayers or biblical passages that you think express Jewish attitudes toward the body or a bodily function.

3. Describe what it means to say that humans are created "in God's image."

4. Think of some beautiful creations that you have seen. Now research the blessing that one traditionally says when seeing a thing of beauty. What difference might there be in your attitude if you look at these beautiful creations as God's creations?

5. List the things that you do to care for yourself and your body. What are some goals that will help improve upon your care?

6. Why do you think many obscene words use or allude to body parts?

7. The Talmud (Babylonian *Sanhedrin* 70a) says that "wine reddens the face of the wicked in this world and whitens it in the world-to-come." Explain what might be meant by this statement.

8. The tale of Hillel and the bathhouse talks about bathing as a religious duty. Have you ever thought of showering or bathing as a religious duty? If you did, in what way might your bathing experience be changed or enhanced?

9. Philo Judaeus wrote that "the body is the soul's house." What do you think he meant?

10. According to the Talmud (*Taanit* 11a), "one who denies oneself proper food is considered a transgressor." What kind of transgression might this be referring to?

11. If you were teaching a unit on Judaism and caring for the body, what suggestions might you have for the class to help them connect proper body care with Jewish thought?

12. Among the many mitzvot to be performed in the morning, there is one that includes washing one's hands upon awakening and reciting the blessing "who has commanded us concerning the washing of the hands." Why do you think the Rabbis ordained that such a blessing be recited first thing in the morning?

13. Calculate how much time you spend per week caring for or about some aspect of your body. Is the amount of time more or less than you would have thought? What do you learn from this?

11. Marriage קִדּוּשִׁין

From the Midrash: Heavenly Mates

A matron once asked Rabbi Yosei ben Chalafta: "What has your God been doing since He finished making the world?"

"He has been matching couples in marriage," was the reply, "the daughter of so and so for so and so; so and so's widow for so and so."

The lady declared that she could do as much as that herself; nothing was easier than to couple any number of slaves with each other.

"You may think it easy," said Rabbi Yosei, "but it is as difficult for God as dividing the Red Sea."

The matron accordingly tried the experiment with a thousand male slaves and as many female slaves, setting them in rows and bidding this man take this woman. The next morning they came to her, one with a broken head, another with gouged-out eyes, a third with a broken leg. One man saying, "I don't want her," and a girl saying, "I don't want him."

Thus was the matron constrained to say that the mating of man and woman was a task not unworthy the intelligence of God.

Midrash, *P'sikta D'Rav Kahana* 11b–12a

אמרה לו ומה הוא יושב ועושה מאותה השעה, אמ' לה מזווג זיווגים, בתו של פלוני לפלוני, אשתו של פל' לפלו', ממונו של פל' לפל'. אמרה והדה היא, אף אני יכולה לעשות כן, כמה עבדים וכמה שפחות יש לי ובשעה קלה אני יכולה לזווגן. א' לה אם קלה היא בעיניך קשה היא לפני הקב"ה כקריעת ים סוף. היניחה ר' יוסי בר' חלפתה והלך לו. מה עשתה, נטלה אלף עבדים ואלף שפחות והעמידה אותן שורות שורות ואמרה, פלן ישא לפלנית פלנית תשא לפלן, וזיווגה אותן בלילה אחד. ובצפרא אתון לגבה, דין רישיה פציע דין עייניה שמיטה דין רגליה תבירא, דין או' לית אנא בעי לדא ודא אמרה לית אני בעי לדין. שלחה והביאה את ר' יוסי בר' חלפתא, אמרה לו אמת היא תורתכם נאה ומשובחת היא על כל מה שאמרת יפה אמרת.

Background of the Tale

In Jewish literature, God is often portrayed as a *shadchan* (matchmaker). The rabbinic tale describes a confrontation between a skeptical Roman matron and Rabbi Yosei ben Chalafta. The Roman matron claimed that she could do the same as God, namely mate and marry off her hundreds of household slaves. It was not long, however, before the newly married couples complained and protested so much that, according to a midrash on this text, the Roman matron admitted that "there was none like Rabbi Yosei's God" [Genesis *Rabbah* 68:4].

Marriage: What Does Judaism Say?

The importance of marriage in Jewish tradition is summed up in the talmudic statement that when one marries, one becomes a complete person. Jewish marriage is regarded as the ideal state. In Genesis 2:18, God tells Adam that it is not good for man to live alone.

Marriage is also a mitzvah, a divine commandment. When a couple marries, it becomes possible for them to fulfill Judaism's first biblical obligation—"be fruitful and multiply." A Jewish marriage celebrates the creation of a new Jewish family. With the arrival of its first child, that family becomes God's partner in the ongoing process of creation. For this reason, the *Zohar* says, "God is constantly creating new worlds by causing marriages to take place" (*Zohar* 1:89a).

The Rabbis use the term *kiddushin* (sanctification) for marriage. This term, related to the root meaning "holy," reflects the spirituality and holiness that are an integral part of the husband-wife relationship.

Of all of the joyous celebrations in the Jewish life cycle, marriage is the ultimate of all joys. The consecration of a marriage is such cause for rejoicing that according to the rabbinic authorities, no other festivity is allowed to interfere with it.

Throughout the ages the Jewish wedding ceremony was an occasion to be shared by the entire Jewish community, and it was the community's responsibility to do everything possible to ensure the happiness of every bride and groom. In many communities in bygone days the festivities continued for the entire week. Even today, many traditional couples celebrate each evening of their first week of marriage in the company of friends and family.

Notable Quotations

1. I will betroth you with righteousness, with justice, with love and compassion. (Hosea 2:21)

2. Love is the responsibility of an I for a Thou. (Martin Buber, *I and Thou*)

3. When a husband and wife are worthy, the *Shechinah* abides with them. (Babylonian Talmud, *Sotah* 17a)

4. Set me as a seal upon your heart. (Song of Songs 8:6)

5. God is constantly creating new worlds by causing marriages to take place. (*Zohar* 1:89a)

6. Grant perfect joy to these loving companions. *(Sheva B'rachot)*

7. Hence a man leaves his father and mother and clings to his wife, so that they become one flesh. (Genesis 2:24)

8. A man who does not have a wife lives without joy, blessing, and goodness. (Babylonian Talmud, *Y'vamot* 62b)

9. Forty days before the creation of a child, a voice proclaims in heaven: "So-and-so's daughter for so-and-so's son." (Babylonian Talmud, *Sotah* 2a)

10. When a man weds his wife who is right for him, the prophet Elijah kisses him and the Holy One loves him. (Babylonian Talmud, *Derech Eretz Zuta* 56a)

11. Rabbi Y'hudah said in the name of Rav: "A man may not marry a woman until he has seen her first." (Babylonian Talmud, *Kiddushin* 41a)

12. One who weds for money will have delinquent offspring. (Talmud, *Kiddushin* 70)

13. From every human being there rises a light that reaches to heaven. When two souls are destined to find each other, their streams of light flow together, and a single brighter light goes forth from their united being. (Baal Shem Tov)

Questions

1. What are three or four of the most important qualities that you would be looking for when searching for a suitable person to marry? Why?

2. What is your opinion of using a professional matchmaker in order to find a suitable mate?

3. What does the Talmud (*Sotah* 17a) mean when it says that "when a husband and wife are worthy, the *Shechinah* abides with them"?

4. According to Jewish tradition, there are several so-called lucky days on which to have your wedding. Research this question to determine Judaism's lucky days for weddings. (Hint: Look at the creation story in the Book of Genesis to see on what day God says it was "very good.")

5. According to the Rabbis, a Jewish marriage affirms that God becomes a third partner. In what way can a couple ensure God's partnership?

6. The *Zohar* (1:89a) states that "God is constantly creating new worlds by causing marriages to take place." How do you understand this statement?

7. According to Deuteronomy 24:5, when a man takes a wife he shall be deferred from military duty. What does this rule say about biblical advice for newlyweds?

12. Stealing and Returning Lost Property לֹא תִּגְנֹב

From the Midrash: Let the Thieves Go

A story is told of a ruler who used to put to death those who received stolen property, but would always let the thieves go. Everybody criticized him for not acting rationally. So what did he do? He had it proclaimed throughout the province, "All people proceed to the arena." Next, what did he do? He brought mice and placed before them portions of food. The mice took the portions and carried them to their holes.

The next day, he again had it proclaimed, "All people proceed to the arena." Again he brought mice and placed before them portions of food, but this time he stopped up the holes, so that when the mice took their food to the holes and found them stopped up, they returned the portions to where they had been. Thus the mice demonstrated that, but for the recipients of stolen goods, there would be no thievery.

Midrash, *Vayikra Rabbah* 6:2

מַעֲשֶׂה בְּשִׁלְטוֹן אֶחָד שֶׁהָיָה הוֹרֵג אֶת הַקַּבְּלָנִין וּמַתִּיר אֶת הַגַּנָּבִים, וְהָיוּ הַכֹּל מַלִּיזִין עָלָיו שֶׁאֵינוּ עוֹשֶׂה כָרָאוּי, מֶה עָשָׂה, הוֹצִיא כָרוֹז בַּמְּדִינָה וְאָמַר: כָּל עַמָּא לַקַמְפּוֹן, מֶה עָשָׂה, הֵבִיא חֻלְדוֹת וְנָתַן לִפְנֵיהֶם מָנוֹת, וְהָיוּ הַחֻלְדוֹת נוֹטְלוֹת אֶת הַמָּנוֹת וּמוֹלִיכוֹת אוֹתָן לַחוֹרִין, לְמָחָר הוֹצִיא כָרוֹז וְאָמַר: כָּל עַמָּא לַקַמְפּוֹן, הֵבִיא חֻלְדוֹת, נָתַן לִפְנֵיהֶן מָנוֹת וְסָתַם אֶת הַחוֹרִים, וְהָיוּ הַחֻלְדוֹת נוֹטְלוֹת אֶת הַמָּנוֹת וּמוֹלִיכוֹת אוֹתָן לַחוֹרִין וּמוֹצְאוֹת אוֹתָן מְסֻתָּמוֹת וּמַחֲזִירוֹת אֶת הַמָּנוֹת לִמְקוֹמָן, לוֹמַר: שֶׁאֵין הַכֹּל אֶלָּא מִן הַקַּבְּלָנִין. הֲרֵי מִן הַשִּׁלְטוֹן.

Background of the Tale

The midrash concerns a popular debate in the Talmud as to who is more guilty, the thief or those who knowingly receive stolen property. In the midrash the ruler is accustomed to putting to death all of those who accept stolen property, but he exonerates the thieves themselves. The people are outraged at the seemingly irrational behavior of the ruler. In order to prove his point, he gathers all of his people to the arena, brings mice, and places before them portions of food. The mice of course take the food and carry it to their mouse holes for eating.

The next day, the ruler again gathers all of the people to the arena and again brings mice and places food before them. This time the ruler puts stops in the holes, so that when the mice take their food to them, they are unable to bring it into the holes. Subsequently they return their food portions to their former place. The ruler thus has taught in this parable that thieves need buyers and receivers of stolen property, and if the receivers of stolen property can be eliminated, then stealing would cease to exist.

Interestingly, the famous talmudic Rabbi Abayei challenges the exoneration of the thief, stating, "If there were no mouse, how would the hole get filled with stolen goods?" (Babylonian Talmud, *Gittin* 45a). In other words, initially there must be a thief in order for there to be stolen property in the first place.

Stealing and Returning Lost Property: What Does Judaism Say?

Theft is a serious transgression in Jewish law, especially in light of it being included among the prohibitions of the Ten Commandments. The Book of Exodus unequivocally commands: "You shall not steal" (Exodus 20:13). Stealing in all forms is far more prevalent in today's society than any of us would care to admit. In any given year thousands upon thousands of towels are "removed" from hotel rooms all around the country. Security experts tell us that among other things, clocks, dishes, furniture, fire extinguishers, and even toilet paper walk away in unprecedented amounts.

In a study of customers' habits in stores, five hundred shoppers were randomly chosen to be observed. Out of that number, an astounding one in twelve stole at least one item!

Government statistics indicate that billions of dollars worth of merchandise is being stolen yearly, in crimes ranging from outright theft to shoplifting, bribery, and fraud.

The Torah has several references to the prohibition of stealing and the penalties involved for doing so. There are also numerous rabbinic texts dealing with stealing. Many of the rabbinic laws concerning damages are cited in the talmudic tractate called *N'zikin*. For example, the *Tosefta* of *Bava Kama* 10:14 says that "one who robs the public must restore to the public. Worse is stealing from the public than stealing from a single individual, for one who steals from an individual can appease that individual and return the theft. The former cannot do this."

There is another kind of theft, the kind that occurs when you deceive another person. In Hebrew this kind of stealing is called *g'neivat daat*, literally "stealing of the mind" of the other person. Among other things, it applies to the bait-and-switch tricks that some retailers utilize when advertising a certain product at a highly reduced price. When interested customers come to the store expecting to purchase the item at the discounted advertised price, the retailer claims that the product is unavailable and substitutes a higher-priced product in its place. Deception of the mind also occurs when a dealer of pre-owned cars dresses up a vehicle or turns back its odometer to make it appear newer.

Cheating is yet another form of stealing, in this case the stealing of a person's ideas. Cheating is on the rise in our society. A recent West Coast study asked thirty thousand college freshmen whether they had ever cheated on a test in their senior year in high school. The results showed that 33 percent said that they had cheated. Today some psychologists say that cheating is inevitable among younger children, because their morality is centered on the idea that whatever brings good or better results is right.

There are also numerous statements in Judaism related to the ethical responsibility of the finder of a lost object. In all cases one can see the Torah's great concern to preserve the sanctity of personal property as well as the ethical duty to return lost property.

Perhaps the truest test of a person's character lies in those border areas of human behavior in which either of two opposed lines of action is defensible. The reaction of one who finds lost property belonging to another is a good case in point. A finder can easily feel tempted to seek an excuse for retaining the lost article without any sense of guilt, even though such a course of action may amount to robbing one's fellow human being. It is for this reason that the Torah considers the return of a lost object to its owner as a religious obligation, a mitzvah. A Jewish person must protect the object found and wait for identification by its rightful owner.

Notable Quotations

1.   If you see your neighbor's ox or sheep gone astray, do not ignore it. You must take it back to your neighbor. If your neighbor does not live near you or you do not know who he is, you shall bring it home and it shall remain with you until your neighbor claims it. (Deuteronomy 22:1–2)

2.   You must not steal, even if it be done merely to annoy, or even to restore double or fourfold or fivefold. Ben Bag Bag said: "You must not steal your own property back from a thief, lest you appear to be stealing." (Midrash *Sifra* 38b)

3.   There are seven kinds of thieves, and the first of them is the one who steals the mind of another human being. Examples of deceivers are the person who urges his neighbor to be his guest when, in his heart, he does not mean to invite him. Or the person who showers gifts upon his neighbor when he knows that his neighbor will not accept them. (*Tosefta, Bava Kama*)

4.   One is forbidden to dye a slave's beard or hair in order to make him appear young. (*Shulchan Aruch, Choshen Mishpat,* Laws of Stealing 358)

Questions

1.   Exodus 21:37 tells us that "if a person steals an ox or a sheep, and kills it or sells it, that person shall pay five oxen for an ox, and four sheep for a sheep." Why would the restitution be different for oxen than for sheep?

2.   There is a separate law in the Torah about returning the lost property of one's enemy. Would you return lost property to a person you greatly disliked? Why do you think that there is a separate law requiring one to return lost things to one's enemy?

3.   The Recanati (thirteenth-century Italian biblical commentator) asks the question: "Of what crime is a thief actually guilty when he commits a theft?" How would you answer this question?

4. If you were writing Jewish law, which of these objects would be considered lost property, and which would be "finders keepers"?

    a. A diamond ring on the street

    b. A coat on the floor of a school gym

    c. A dog in a forest

    d. A charm bracelet washing up on a beach

    e. A dollar bill on a bank floor

5. Several years ago the *New York Times* reported that the Soviet Union has been holding important works of art that it seized from Nazi Germany and has been showing them in various Russian art galleries. The problem is that Germany wants the paintings back, along with many other works of art that it had lost. To make matters even more awkward for the Soviet Union, Germany has given post–Communist Russia more than fifty billion dollars in aid, and it would like some thanks. Further complicating the case, the Red Army grabbed not only German state property, but private collections the Nazis stole from Jews. These too, Germany argues, ought to be returned to their rightful owners if their heirs can be found. How do you think Jewish law would rule on this matter? Should the Soviet Union return these items to Germany, or ought they be able to keep them as reparations for the vast damage that the invading German army wreaked on the Soviet Union's museums? (Note: International conventions adopted in 1954 and 1970 state that in times of war, artwork should not be destroyed and, if expatriated, should be returned.) At least one country has recently complied. Iraq was forced to return what it took from Kuwait's museums in 1990.

6. If you were taking a test and saw the student sitting next to you glancing over at your paper, what would you do?

7. Can you think of a situation when cheating might be morally permissible?

8. Do you think that it is possible for a parent or teacher to teach a child the value of not stealing or cheating and the importance of living a life of honesty? Choose a partner and share your ideas about how to go about instilling the value of honesty in another person.

9. Read the following quotation:

What is considered lost property? If one found a donkey or a cow grazing on the way, this is not lost property. If one, however, finds a donkey and its burden topsy-turvy or a cow running through a vineyard, this is obviously lost property.

Mishnah Bava M'tzia 2:9

Explain this quotation in your own words.

10. Read the following quotation:

The following articles belong to the finder: if one finds scattered fruit, scattered money, small sheaves in a public thoroughfare, round cakes of pressed figs, a baker's loaves, strings of fish, pieces of meat, fleeces of wool that have been brought from the country, bundles of flax, and strips of purple, colored wool—all these belong to the finder.

Mishnah Bava M'tzia 2:1

Why do you think that all of the above articles ought to belong to the finder? What do they all have in common?

13. Ecology בַּל תַּשְׁחִית

From the Midrash: Do Not Destroy the Earth

*W*hen God created Adam,
God led him around the Garden of Eden
and said to him: "Behold my works.
See how wonderful and beautiful they
are. All that I have created, for your
sake did I create it. Now see to it that
you do not spoil and destroy my world,
for if you do, there will be no one to
repair it after you."

Midrash, *Kohelet Rabbah* 7:13

בְּשעה שברא הקב"ה את
אדם הראשון נטלו והחזירו על כל
אילני גן עדן ואמר לו ראה מעשי
כמה נאים ומשובחין הן וכל מה
שבראתי בשבילך בראתי, תן דעתך
שלא תקלקל ותחריב את עולמי,
שאם קלקלת אין מי שיתקן אחריך.

Background of the Tale

This midrash, with its message of not despoiling the earth, relates to the perfection of the beautiful Garden of Eden. According to the midrash, God took Adam on a tour of the Garden of Eden to see its beauty. In Genesis 1:28, Adam and Eve are told to be fruitful and multiply, filling the earth and subduing it. Although they were told to master the earth, the midrash cautions that they must be careful not to needlessly destroy the environment, for there will be no one who comes afterward to repair it. Adam and Eve and all humans to follow are given the task of being the stewards of the world, the protectors of the environment. The understanding here is that God has put people in the world to make use of it, not to exploit it. How the Jewish people interact with the environment is part of our very mission as Jews.

Ecology: What Does Judaism Say?

The midrash above reflects the text taken from Deuteronomy 20:19: "When you wage war against a city, and you have to besiege it in order to capture it, do not destroy its trees, wielding an ax against them. You may eat from them, but you must not cut them down." The rabbinic principle here is known as *bal tashchit,* "do not destroy." From the verse that forbids the cutting down of fruit-bearing trees, the ancient Sages extended the principle to prohibiting willful destruction of any object from which someone might benefit.

Today the problem of ecology is more severe than in centuries past. Global wars, the invention of the diesel engine, the use of nuclear energy, and building activities on a scale unimagined in the past have brought environmental plagues into the world. Water and air pollution, toxic chemicals, ozone destruction, soil erosion, and deforestation are modern-day plagues that were unknown in biblical times.

Deuteronomy 23:13–15 mandates the proper disposal of sewage in the context of its own time: "There shall be an area for you outside the camp, where you may relieve yourself. With your gear you shall have a spike, and when you have squatted you shall dig a hole with it and cover up your excrement."

The principle of *bal tashchit* (do not destroy) serves as the basis for the talmudic law that prohibits willful destruction of natural resources or any kind of vandalism, even if the act is committed by the owners of the property. According to this law, one must not destroy anything that may be useful to others. According to the Babylonian Talmud (*Shabbat* 105a), persons who tear their clothing, smash their furniture in a fit of anger, or squander their money are likened to an idolater. Just as one must be careful not to destroy or injure one's own body, one must be careful not to destroy or injure one's own property. Whoever breaks a utensil or spoils any other thing that is fit for human enjoyment breaks the command "do not destroy."

Waste disposal was a major problem in rabbinic times. Care was taken that bits of broken glass should not be scattered on public land where they would cause injury. We are told that saintly men would bury their broken glassware deep in their own fields (Babylonian Talmud, *Bava Kama* 30a).

Showing disrespect to food is also singled out in the Talmud for special attention. For example, one is not allowed to throw bread, nor is one allowed to pass a cup full of liquid over bread. In both cases, the bread could be ruined (Babylonian Talmud, *B'rachot* 50b). Bread especially receives attention because traditionally it represents the essence of food.

Rabbi Samson Raphael Hirsch, one of the founders of modern Orthodoxy, summarizes the mainstream approach that balances natural preservation with legitimate human needs:

> Do not destroy anything is the first and most general call of God, which comes to you, humanity, when you realize yourself as master of the earth. God's call proclaims to you: If you destroy, if you ruin—at that moment you are not human. You are an animal, and you have no right to the things around you. I lent them to you for wise use only. Never forget that I lent them to you.
>
> *Horeb: A Philosophy of Jewish Law and Observances*

In this passage, Hirsch asserts the importance of the wise use of God's creation, while offering a stern rebuke against abuse of the earth and its resources. Wasteful destruction is a transgression both against God and humanity.

To sum up, Jewish law requires that its people not merely refrain from polluting the environment. Rather, they must be proactive and take affirmative action to clean up the world and keep it safe for generations to come. They are to be active guardians of the world and all that it contains.

Notable Quotations

1. Whoever destroys anything that could be useful to another person breaks the law of *bal tashchit*. (Babylonian Talmud, *Kodashim* 32a)

2. Threshing floors must be kept far enough away from a town to prevent the husks of grain and grasses from polluting the air of the town when the wind blows. (*Mishnah Bava Batra* 2:8)

3. Do not dump waste in any place from which it could be scattered by the wind or spread by flooding. (*Mishneh Torah,* Tamid and Musaf Offerings 2:15)

4. Furnaces and other causes of smoke, odor, and air pollution are not permitted inside a city. (Babylonian Talmud, *Bava Kama* 82b)

5. Whoever tears garments in anger, breaks vessels in anger, and scatters money in anger, regard that person as an idolater. (Babylonian Talmud, *Shabbat* 105b)

6. It is forbidden to live in a town that does not have a green garden. (Jerusalem Talmud, *Kiddushin* 4:12)

7. Rabbi Yochanan ben Zakkai used to say: If you have a sapling in your hand and someone should say to you that the Messiah has come, stay and complete the planting, and then go to greet the Messiah. (Babylonian Talmud, *Avot D'Rabbi Natan* 31b)

8. Rabbi Shimon bar Yochai said: Three things are of equal importance: earth, humans, and rain. (Midrash, *B'reishit Rabbah* 13:3)

9. Land, like humans and animals, must have time to rest, to renew itself. The Torah teaches, "Six years you shall plant your field, . . . but in the seventh year the land shall have a Sabbath of complete rest, a Sabbath of the Lord." You shall neither sow your field nor prune your vineyard. (Leviticus 25:3–5)

10. Even if the land is full of good things, you must still plant. Even if you are old, you must plant. (*Midrash Tanchuma, Kodashim* 8)

11. One who buys a tree from a friend for felling shall cut it in such a way that the stump remains from which a new tree can grow. (Babylonian Talmud, *Bava Batra* 80b)

12. If a person kills a tree before its time, it is as though a soul has been murdered. (Nachman of Bratzlav)

Questions

1. In the Talmud (*Shabbat* 105), one who tears garments and breaks vessels is compared to an idolater. What is the message of this comparison? Do you agree with it? Why or why not?

2. Deuteronomy 20:19 asks the question: "Are trees of the field human?" In what ways do you think trees are similar to human beings? How do they differ?

3. What are some ways in which we waste natural resources in our homes, schools, and synagogues?

4. Some environmentalists have said that all of a person's actions have consequences that will affect the environment. Do you agree?

5. The mitzvah of *bal tashchit* teaches the importance of not being wasteful. List some suggestions that would help people conserve and be less wasteful in their lives.

6. Explain the moral of this story from the Babylonian Talmud (*Taanit* 23a):

> A rabbi was passing through a field when he noticed an elderly man planting an acorn.
> "Why are you planting that acorn?" he asked. "Do you expect to live long enough to see it grow into an oak tree?"
> The man answered, "My grandparents planted seeds so that I might enjoy the shade and the fruit trees. Now I do likewise for my grandchildren and all those who come after me."

7. In your opinion, was the world made for us, or were we made for it? Explain your answer.

8. Do human beings bear the sole responsibility for the quality of life on earth? Why or why not?

9. Do you think the statement in the midrash of *Kohelet Rabbah* "do not ruin my world" means "leave it as it is"? In your opinion, is land that is untouched by human activity always better in some way than inhabited land? Explain your answer.

10. How can observance of Shabbat make any difference in how people treat the environment during the rest of the week?

11. What did Nachman of Bratzlav mean when he said that "if a person kills a tree before its time, it is as though a soul has been murdered"?

12. The poet Solomon ibn Gabirol once said that "the world is a tree and human beings its fruit." What does this statement mean? Do you agree with it? Why or why not?

13. The Torah itself is called a "tree of life" *(eitz chayim)*. Why do you think this is so?

14. Jewish mystics believe that the outer world of nature is a mirror of people's inner nature. In what way do you think that the more you learn about nature, the more you can know about yourself?

15. Research prayers in the *siddur* that display God's power in nature and in the environment. What do you think is the purpose of including such prayers in the prayer book?

14. Old Age כְּבוֹד זְקֵנִים

From the Talmud: Honoring the Elderly

*R*abbi Y'hudah says: Be careful
to respect an old man who has forgotten
his knowledge through no fault of his own,
for it was said: both the whole tablets and
the fragments of the tablets were placed
in the Ark.

Babylonian Talmud, *B'rachot* 8b

רַבִּי יְהוּדָה אוֹמֵר: עַד שֶׁיִּשְׁחוֹט

אֶת הַוְּרִידִין, וְהִזָּהֲרוּ בְּזָקֵן שֶׁשָּׁכַח

תַּלְמוּדוֹ מֵחֲמַת אוּנְסוֹ, דְּאָמְרִינַן:

לוּחוֹת וְשִׁבְרֵי לוּחוֹת מוּנָּחוֹת בָּאָרוֹן.

Background of the Tale

This tale concerns a talmudic debate, in which Rabbi Y'hoshua ben Levi, using a
teaching of Rabbi Y'hudah, is careful to remind his children of the importance of
honoring one's elders and to therefore support the ruling of the elderly and ailing Rabbi
Y'hudah. By this time Rabbi Y'hudah's health has begun to fail, and he is prone to many
lapses in memory. He reminds everyone, using the legend of the broken tablets, that he is
still of value to the community and ought not to be discarded. In the legend of the
broken tablets upon which this tale draws, Moses drops the tablets to the ground after
watching in horror the revelry of the Israelite people dancing around the Golden Calf
that they have built and are worshiping. Jewish legend has it that the broken tablets were
not discarded, but out of respect and honor to them they too, along with the new set of
tablets, were carried in the Ark of the Covenant as the Israelites wandered through the
desert for forty years.

Old Age: What Does Judaism Say?

Consider the words of Leviticus 19:32: "Rise before the aged and show respect to the elderly." This passage teaches the mitzvah of *hidur p'nei zakein* (respect for the elders) and teaches that one must treat older adults with respect and dignity. The phrase in Hebrew is often posted in buses in the State of Israel, where people are encouraged to give up their seat for an elderly person.

Throughout Jewish history, the elders of the Israelite community were sought out for advice because they had participated in so many of life's experiences and were respected because of this fact.

When the aged needed support to live independently and the family lacked the necessary resources, the Jewish community always came to the rescue and provided assistance. Yet it was not until modern times that the elderly capable of independence were treated as a group separate from the sick and the poor in the community. Thus, societies for the aged and homes for the elderly developed in North America in the nineteenth century. The first Jewish home for the aged in the United States was established in St. Louis in 1855. Today most cities that boast substantial Jewish communities have care facilities for the elderly. Many synagogues and Jewish community centers today have special programs for older adults, providing them with continued opportunities for study, socializing, and continued growth as human beings and as contributing members of the Jewish community.

Perhaps the whole philosophy of care for the aged can be summed up in the poignant cry of Psalm 71:9: "Cast me not off in the time of old age. When my strength fails, do not forsake me."

Notable Quotations

1. Even the chirping of a bird awakens the aged. (Babylonian Talmud, *Shabbat* 152a)

2. How welcome is old age. The aged are beloved by God. (Midrash, *Sh'mot Rabbah* 5:12)

3. Rabbi Yosei the Galilean said, "To honor the aged means that one should not sit in the seat of an elderly person, nor speak before he has spoken, nor contradict him." (Babylonian Talmud, *Kiddushin* 32b)

4. Even in old age they shall bear fruit, they shall be full of vigor and strength. (Psalm 92:15)

5. The prosperity of a country is in accordance with its treatment of the elderly. (Nachman of Bratzlav)

6. When we were young, we were treated as men. Now that we have grown, we are looked upon as babies. (Babylonian Talmud, *Bava Kama* 92b)

7. As regards scholars, the older they become, the more wisdom they acquire. But as regards the ignorant, the older they become, the more foolish they become. (Babylonian Talmud, *Shabbat* 152a)

8. "You shall rise before the aged" means any aged. Rabbi Yochanan used to rise in the presence of aged non-Jews, saying, "How many experiences have happened to these people." (Babylonian Talmud, *Kiddushin* 33a)

Questions

1. Read the following story from the Talmud.

> *The students of Rabbi Zeira, and some say Rabbi Ada bar Ahavah, asked him: "In virtue of what have you succeeded in reaching such old age?"*
>
> *He answered them: "In all my days, I never showed them impatience in my house. I never walked in front of any person greater than me, I never thought about Torah matters while walking in dirty alleys, I never walked four paces without musing over the Torah or without wearing t'fillin, I never slept in the house of study, either a full night's sleep or even a nap, I never rejoiced in my neighbor's shame, and I never called my fellow by an [embarrassing] nickname."*
>
> Babylonian Talmud, *Taanit* 20b

What is the moral of the story? Do you have a personal recipe for attaining old age? What is it, and why?

2. It is written in the Talmud (*Sanhedrin* 36b) that we do not seat as a judge in the Sanhedrin an old man or a eunuch or one who is childless. Can you think of an explanation for this ruling?

3. We are told in the Passover Haggadah that when Rabbi Elazar was seventeen years old he said, "I appear like a person who is seventy years old." What do you think motivated him to make this statement? Do his words reflect a positive or negative attitude toward growing older?

4. What is your opinion of the way in which older people are portrayed in movies and on television?

5. Job 12:12 says that "with the aged comes wisdom, and length of days brings understanding." Do you agree? Why or why not?

6. What is your opinion of retirement communities that do not allow families with young children to live in them? Why?

7. Explain this statement from *Pirkei Avot* 4:25: "Elisha ben Avuyah said, 'When a person learns something while still young, it is similar to ink written on new paper. However, when a person learns something as an older person, it is like writing with ink on paper that has already been erased.'"

8. What kinds of things could a synagogue or Jewish community center do in order to provide a more supportive environment for older adult members?

9. Here is a riddle by Rabbi Yosei ben Kisma in which he expresses the hardship of old age: "Two are better than three, and woe for the one thing that goes and does not return." Can you solve this riddle? To what was Rabbi Yosei referring? What is "the one thing that goes" in old age, never to return?

10. What are various ways in which one can give honor to the elderly?

11. What are some special things that grandchildren might choose to do for grandparents to show them the special honor that Judaism recommends? If you have grandparents, how have you shown them honor?

15. Honoring the Dead and Comforting Mourners
כְּבוּד הַמֵת

From the Talmud: Rich and Poor in Death

*O*ur Rabbis taught: *Formerly they were wont to convey victuals to the house of mourning, the rich in silver and gold baskets, and the poor in baskets of peeled willow twigs, and the poor felt shamed. They therefore instituted that all should convey victuals in osier baskets of peeled willow twigs out of deference to the poor.*

Our Rabbis taught: Formerly they were wont to serve drinks in a house of mourning, the rich in white glass vessels and the poor in colored glass, and the poor felt shamed. They therefore instituted that all should serve drinks in colored glass, out of deference to the poor.

Formerly they were wont to uncover the face of the rich and cover the face of the poor, because their faces turned livid in years of drought, and the poor felt shamed. They therefore instituted that everybody's face should be covered out of deference to the poor.

תָּנוּ רַבָּנַן: בָּרִאשׁוֹנָה הָיוּ מוֹלִיכִין בְּבֵית הָאֵבֶל, עֲשִׁירִים – בְּקַלָתוֹת שֶׁל כֶּסֶף וְשֶׁל זָהָב, וַעֲנִיִּים – בְּסַלֵּי נְצָרִים שֶׁל עֲרָבָה קְלוּפָה. וְהָיוּ עֲנִיִּים מִתְבַּיְּישִׁים, הִתְקִינוּ שֶׁיְּהוּ הַכֹּל מְבִיאִין בְּסַלֵּי נְצָרִים שֶׁל עֲרָבָה קְלוּפָה, מִפְּנֵי כְבוֹדָן שֶׁל עֲנִיִּים. תָּנוּ רַבָּנַן: בָּרִאשׁוֹנָה הָיוּ מַשְׁקִין בְּבֵית הָאֵבֶל, עֲשִׁירִים – בִּזְכוּכִית לְבָנָה, וַעֲנִיִּים – בִּזְכוּכִית צְבוּעָה, וְהָיוּ עֲנִיִּים מִתְבַּיְּישִׁין. הִתְקִינוּ שֶׁיְּהוּ הַכֹּל מַשְׁקִין בִּזְכוּכִית צְבוּעָה, מִפְּנֵי כְבוֹדָן שֶׁל עֲנִיִּים. בָּרִאשׁוֹנָה הָיוּ מְגַלִּין פְּנֵי עֲשִׁירִים וּמְכַסִּין פְּנֵי עֲנִיִּים, מִפְּנֵי שֶׁהָיוּ מוּשְׁחָרִין פְּנֵיהֶן מִפְּנֵי בַּצֹּרֶת, וְהָיוּ עֲנִיִּים מִתְבַּיְּישִׁין. הִתְקִינוּ שֶׁיְּהוּ מְכַסִּין פְּנֵי הַכֹּל, מִפְּנֵי כְבוֹדָן שֶׁל עֲנִיִּים. בָּרִאשׁוֹנָה הָיוּ מוֹצִיאָין עֲשִׁירִים בְּדַרְגָּשׁ, וַעֲנִיִּים בִּכְלִיכָה, וְהָיוּ עֲנִיִּים מִתְבַּיְּישִׁין, הִתְקִינוּ שֶׁיְּהוּ הַכֹּל מוֹצִיאָין בִּכְלִיכָה, מִפְּנֵי כְבוֹדָן שֶׁל עֲנִיִּים. בָּרִאשׁוֹנָה הָיוּ מַנִּיחִין אֶת הַמּוּגְמָר תַּחַת חוֹלֵי מֵעַיִם מֵתִים, וְהָיוּ

Formerly they were wont to bring out the rich for burial on an ornamented bed, and the poor on a plain bier, and the poor felt shamed. They instituted therefore that all should be brought out on a plain bier out of deference to the poor.

Formerly the expense of taking the dead out to one's burial fell harder on one's near-of-kin than one's own death so that the dead person's near-of-kin abandoned and fled, until at last Rabban Gamliel came forward and, disregarding his own dignity, came out to his burial in flaxen vestments. Said Rav Papa: And nowadays all the world should follow the practice of coming out even in a paltry shroud that costs but a zuz.

Babylonian Talmud, *Mo-eid Katan* 27a–b

חוֹלֵי מֵעַיִם חַיִּים מִתְבַּיְּישִׁין, הִתְקִינוּ שֶׁיְּהוּ מַנִּיחִין תַּחַת הַכֹּל, מִפְּנֵי כְבוֹדָן שֶׁל חוֹלֵי מֵעַיִם חַיִּים. בָּרִאשׁוֹנָה הָיוּ מַטְבִּילִין אֶת הַכֵּלִים עַל גַּבֵּי נִדּוֹת מֵתוֹת, וְהָיוּ נִדּוֹת חַיּוֹת מִתְבַּיְּישׁוֹת, הִתְקִינוּ שֶׁיְּהוּ מַטְבִּילִין עַל גַּבֵּי כָל הַנָּשִׁים, מִפְּנֵי כְבוֹדָן שֶׁל נִדּוֹת חַיּוֹת. בָּרִאשׁוֹנָה מַטְבִּילִין עַל גַּבֵּי זָבִין מֵתִים, וְהָיוּ זָבִין חַיִּים מִתְבַּיְּישִׁין. הִתְקִינוּ שֶׁיְּהוּ מַטְבִּילִין עַל גַּב הַכֹּל, מִפְּנֵי כְבוֹדָן שֶׁל זָבִין חַיִּים. בָּרִאשׁוֹנָה הָיְתָה הוֹצָאַת הַמֵּת קָשָׁה לִקְרוֹבָיו יוֹתֵר מִמִּיתָתוֹ, עַד שֶׁהָיוּ קְרוֹבָיו מַנִּיחִין אוֹתוֹ וּבוֹרְחִין. עַד שֶׁבָּא רַבָּן גַּמְלִיאֵל וְנָהַג קַלּוּת רֹאשׁ בְּעַצְמוֹ וְיָצָא בִּכְלֵי פִשְׁתָּן, וְנָהֲגוּ הָעָם אַחֲרָיו לָצֵאת בִּכְלֵי פִשְׁתָּן. אָמַר רַב פַּפָּא: וְהָאִידָנָא נְהוּג עָלְמָא אֲפִילוּ בִּצְרָדָא בַּר זוּזָא.

Background of the Tale

This tale, written many centuries ago, details the customs and practices of preparing the dead for burial and the differences that had been established regarding the rich and the poor. It appears that the deceased of a rich family were able to be provided by their loved ones with a more luxurious preparation. For example, when food was brought to the house of mourning for the meal of condolence, the family of the rich would bring silver and gold baskets, while the poor brought baskets of willow twigs. The rich would serve beverages in the house of shivah in white glass vessels, while the poor could only afford colored glass. Because of the high value that Judaism has always placed on not shaming others, it was decided by the rabbinic community that out of deference to the poor, all should be treated in the most simple and plain fashion possible. At the end of the tale, Rabban Gamliel, the preeminent leader of his generation, and himself a wealthy man, left orders that his body be carried to the grave in a simple linen garment. Since coffins were not used at that time in Jewish funerals, all passersby could see the simple garment in which Rabban Gamliel was interred. From then on, everyone followed Rabban Gamliel's example.

Jewish custom today is that both rich and poor are treated with equal respect when death arrives. A belief in the democracy of death has shaped Jewish funeral and burial customs so that they are simple and unostentatious. The religious prescription of a wooden casket is meant to avoid ostentation at the funeral, and the simple traditional white linen garment in which the deceased are dressed symbolizes the democracy and equality of death—there is no distinction between the rich and the poor, and all are equal in the eyes of God.

Honoring the Dead and Comforting Mourners: What Does Judaism Say?

The deceased is accorded a great deal of honor as the family begins to plan for the funeral and burial. Preserving the dignity of life and of the human body sets the tone for the Jewish response to death. Historically, every family had the responsibility to care for its own dead. Today, in many Jewish communities that have Conservative and Orthodox synagogues, this task has been assumed by a group of caring men and women called the *chevrah kadisha* (holy burial society) or sometimes called *chevrah k'vod hamet* (the society for the honor of the deceased). Many Reform synagogues do not have an actual *chevrah kadisha,* and for them the funeral home usually does all the preparation. However, most Reform synagogues do have a group called the caring committee. This group of people, who are among the first to be informed of a death in the community, are generally familiar with Jewish funerary practices and help the mourners prepare their loved one for burial.

Just as a baby is washed and enters the world clean and pure, so does a Jewish person leave the world cleansed by the religious act of *taharah,* "purification." Caring for the body from the time of death until burial is considered an act of ultimate kindness and generosity, since it can never be repaid by the recipient.

The Talmud records that at one time the bodies of the wealthy were brought to burial on a richly ornamented stately bed, while the bodies of the poor were brought to burial on a platform (Babylonian Talmud, *Mo-eid Katan* 27a–b). This practice brought embarrassment to the poor, resulting in a law requiring all dead, rich and poor alike, to be brought to burial on a plain platform. To this day, the deceased is customarily dressed in white, plain linen shrouds.

According to Jewish tradition, the deceased is shown honor by not being left alone before the funeral. In traditional settings, a *shomeir* (literally, "watchperson") will stay with the deceased from the time of death until burial. A candle is placed near the deceased, and the *shomeir* often reads Psalms. It is a Jewish sign of respect that the deceased never be left alone.

Jewish tradition frowns upon the viewing of the body. Although it has become the widespread American custom in non-Jewish settings to have the body on exhibition the night before the funeral or to have an open casket during the funeral, this practice is contrary to Judaism. The dead are not to be put on display. Thus Judaism encourages us to remember our loved ones in the vibrancy of their life rather than in death. In addition, Judaism requires that a person be buried within twenty-four hours after death unless there are extenuating circumstances.

Jewish law requires that the casket be made entirely of wood, with no metal, nails, or hinges allowed. When buried, this allows for the casket to return naturally to the earth. Simple, unostentatious caskets have always been preferred in Jewish tradition. The use of flowers to adorn the casket is also discouraged. Instead, well-wishers are encouraged to give *tzedakah* in memory of the deceased as a lasting memorial.

The Hebrew word for "funeral" is *l'vayah*, literally meaning "to accompany." This teaches that a Jewish funeral requires community involvement. It is a mitzvah and an act of respect to attend the funeral service. At the funeral, the custom is to deliver a eulogy that delineates the attributes of the deceased. It is considered an honor and an important obligation for mourners and family members to provide insights for the eulogy.

It is an act of respect and honor to walk alongside the casket at the cemetery as it makes its way to the burial plot. The custom is for the family to choose relatives and close friends to act as pallbearers. At the cemetery, at the end of the brief service, it is a religious duty for relatives and friends to help shovel the earth back into the grave to cover the casket. As difficult as this may seem, it is literally the last physical act that family and friends can perform for the deceased and helps start the mourners on their way to acceptance and healing.

It is an important religious duty to visit mourners, especially during the week after the death of their loved one. The custom of offering consolation to the bereaved is an ancient one. In the Bible, when Job's children died, his three close friends came to visit him. In Job 2:13, we are told that they "sat with him on the ground seven days and seven nights. None spoke a word to him for they saw how great was his suffering." The behavior of these closest friends of Job has become the model for the way in which Jews are to act in a house of mourning.

During shivah, the period of seven days of mourning, friends and members of the community come and formally express their condolences. Many people are uncomfortable in a house of shivah and are not exactly sure of what to say, searching for just the right words. In fact, they may be inclined not to speak until spoken to, and this is exactly what Jewish tradition instructs. Visitors are to support the mourner, even in silence. A warm embrace or an arm around the shoulders is a wonderful nonverbal message to the bereaved.

Visitors who do converse with the mourners should remember that they are not expected to cheer them up in their time of anguish. One does not console by attempting to distract the mourners. They find greatest comfort in talking about their dear ones who have passed on, by recalling meaningful incidents in their lives that were not known or may have been forgotten by the family. When speaking of the deceased and reminiscing, a Hebrew phrase is generally added: *alav hashalom* (may he rest in peace) or *aleha hashalom* (may she rest in peace). *Zichrono livrachah* (for a male) and *zichronah livrachah* (for a female) are also used, meaning "of blessed memory."

The traditional statement of condolence to the mourners is *HaMakom y'nacheim etchem b'toch sh'ar aveilei Tziyon virushalayim,* "May God comfort you among the mourners for Zion and Jerusalem."

At the end of the first thirty days (known as *sh'loshim*) after the death of a person, it is appropriate for family and friends to gather together to read or study appropriate texts and to speak about the deceased in his or her honor. There are also times during the year that have been set aside as special for grave visitation.

Jewish tradition has added a special ritual to help mourners meet the crisis of bereavement and annually honor their loved ones. This is the annual commemoration of the anniversary of death known as *yahrzeit*. Each year, on the anniversary of the death, a special day is consecrated to one's loved one. The *yahrzeit* begins with the lighting of a twenty-four-hour candle on the night of the anniversary. Light is symbolic of a person's soul, suggesting immortality. On the day of the *yahrzeit* itself, the traditional custom is to attend worship services and recite the Mourner's *Kaddish*. Appropriate too is the fulfillment of some mitzvah in honor of the deceased on the day of the *yahrzeit*. This might consist of Torah study and contributing to some worthy cause. It is also appropriate for family and friends to gather on the *yahrzeit* for the purpose of recalling various aspects of the life of their loved one, thereby perpetuating his or her memory in a warm and loving family atmosphere.

Finally, the association of memorial services with important holy days is very characteristic of Judaism. On Yom Kippur, Sh'mini Atzeret, Passover, and Shavuot, a remembrance service called *Yizkor* takes place. This service allows participants to remember and honor their loved ones and the values they cherished and transmitted while alive. In this way they are encouraged to continue to lead the good lives that their loved ones bequeathed to them. As with a *yahrzeit,* it is also customary to kindle a twenty-four-hour candle on the evening preceding *Yizkor.* The custom is also to pledge charity and perform other kind deeds to honor the memory of the departed.

Notable Quotations

1. When a person sheds tears at the death of a virtuous person, the Holy One counts them and places them in His treasure house. (Babylonian Talmud, *Shabbat* 105a)

2. Silence is meritorious in the house of mourning. (Babylonian Talmud, *Berachot* 6b)

3. Kindness that is done for the dead is a true act of kindness, since one does it without expectation of any repayment. (Rashi on Genesis 47:29)

4. Rabbi Shimon the son of Elazar said: "Do not appease your fellow in the hour of his anger, and do not comfort him when his dead lies before him, and do not question him in the hour of his vow, and do not strive to see him in the hour of his disgrace." (*Pirkei Avot* 4:23)

5. Rabbi Yochanan said: "Comforters are not allowed to say a word until the mourner begins the conversation." (Babylonian Talmud, *Mo-eid Katan* 28b)

6. It seems to me that the duty of comforting mourners takes precedence over the duty of visiting the sick, because comforting mourners is an act of benevolence toward the living and the dead. (Maimonides, *Mishneh Torah*, Laws of Mourning 14:7)

7. A person who meets a mourner after one year and consoles him, to what can he be compared? To a physician who meets a person whose leg had broken and healed, and says to him, "Let me break your leg again, and reset it, to convince you that my treatment was good." (Babylonian Talmud, *Mo-eid Katan* 21b)

8. Rabbi Yosei the son of Rabbi Bun said: "Those who are standing in the presence of the dead at a funeral are not standing in honor of the deceased, but in honor of those who are performing an act of kindness for the deceased." (Jerusalem Talmud, *Bikurim* 3:3)

9. Rabbi Yochanan said in the name of Rabbi Shimon ben Yochai: "What is the proof that the person who keeps the dead unburied overnight transgresses a negative commandment? The biblical verse 'His body shall not remain overnight...you shall bury him the same day' [Deuteronomy 21:23]." (Babylonian Talmud, *Sanhedrin* 46b)

10. If a person is near death, it is forbidden to leave him, so that he should not die alone. (*Shulchan Aruch, Yoreh Dei-ah* 339:4)

11. One who sees a corpse en route to burial and does not accompany it is like one who mocks the poor and deserves excommunication. He should accompany the corpse for a distance of at least four cubits. (*Shulchan Aruch, Yoreh Dei-ah* 361:3)

Questions

1. Read the story from the midrash on Proverbs 31:10 and answer the questions that follow.

> While Rabbi Meir was teaching in the *beit midrash* on a Sabbath afternoon, his two sons died. What did their mother do? She left them lying on their couch and spread a sheet over them. When the Sabbath ended, Rabbi Meir returned and asked: "Where are my sons?"
>
> "They went to the house of study," Beruriah answered.
>
> "I looked for them but I did not see them."
>
> She gave him the cup of wine for *Havdalah,* and he pronounced the blessing. Again he inquired, "Where are my two sons?"
>
> "They must have gone elsewhere and will return soon." She brought him food, and after he ate she said, "I have a question for you."
>
> "Ask," he said.
>
> "A while ago a man came and left with me an item to watch for him. Now he has returned to claim what he left. Shall I give it back to him or not?"
>
> "Is not one who holds a deposit required to return it to its owner?" Rabbi Meir asked.
>
> "Still, without your opinion," Beruriah said, "I would not give it back to him."
>
> What did she do then? She took him by the hand and led him up to the children's room and brought him to the couch. She pulled off the sheet, and he saw that both boys were dead. He burst into tears.
>
> Then Beruriah said to him, "Did you not tell me that we are required to restore a pledge to the owner?"
>
> To which he answered, "'*Adonai* has given and *Adonai* has taken away; blessed be the name of *Adonai.*'" (Job 1:21)
>
> Midrash Proverbs 31:10

What is the moral of this story? Why did Beruriah not tell her husband immediately of the death of the two children? Do you think she was helpful to her husband? Why or why not?

2. Why do you think that the ancient Sages regarded the preparation of a person for burial as one of the ultimate acts of kindness? Can you think of other things that one might do for another that would be put in the same category?

3. Rabbi Yochanan taught centuries ago that comforters should not say a word at a house of shivah until the mourners begin the conversation. What do you think motivated Rabbi Yochanan to make this remark? Do you agree with it? Why or why not?

4. The traditional words of comfort to the bereaved are "May God comfort you among the mourners for Zion and Jerusalem." Why do you think that it is necessary to add in the phrase "for Zion and Jerusalem"?

5. What are some of the things that you think one ought to include in a letter of condolence to a mourner?

6. Have you ever been to a shivah at a house of mourning? How did it feel to be there? Describe the behavior of the people. Was the mood solemn as you had expected it to be? What is your opinion of the talmudic advice that "silence is meritorious in the house of mourning" (Babylonian Talmud, *B'rachot* 6b)?

7. Why do you think that Judaism has created so many different rituals related to death and dying? Which rituals do you think are most helpful to the bereaved? Are there any rituals that you find difficult to understand?

8. Do you think family members should be encouraged to speak at the funeral of their loved ones? Why or why not?

9. Do you have any suggestions for explaining death and dying to a young child?

10. Have you ever watched someone in your family light a *yahrzeit* candle on the anniversary of the death of their loved one? If so, how did the lighting of the candle make you feel? Why do you think that Jewish custom is to light a candle on a *yahrzeit* or before a *Yizkor* service? What kinds of feelings do people have when they watch the flickering of a candle?

11. Many Reform synagogues have a custom of the entire congregation rising and joining in the Mourner's *Kaddish*. What is your feeling about this custom? What are the benefits to those in mourning to have everyone rise and join in the mourner's prayer? What are the disadvantages?

16. Speech and Language לָשׁוֹן הָרָע

From the Midrash: Tale of the Two Tongues

A rabbi sent his servant to the market with the general instruction, "Buy the best thing there that one can eat." The servant returned with a tongue. Later, the rabbi asked him to go back to the market to buy the worst thing that one could eat. The servant again came back with a tongue.

"What is with you?" asked the rabbi. "Here I've asked you to buy both the best and the worst, and you come back with a couple of tongues."

"That's true," responded the servant. "After all, cannot a tongue be one of the best things in the world and an evil tongue be one of the worst?"

Midrash, *Vayikra Rabbah* 33:1

אַרשב"ג לְטָבִי עַבְדֵיה: פּוּק זְבֵין לִי צֵדוּ טָבָא מִן שׁוּקָא, נְפַק זְבַן לֵיה לִישָׁן. א"ל פּוּק זְבֵין לִי צֵדוּ בִּישָׁא מִן שׁוּקָא, נְפַק זְבַן לֵיה לִישָׁן. א"ל: מַהוּ דֵין, דְּכַד אֲנָא אָמַר לָךְ צֵדוּ טָבָא אַתְּ זְבַן לִי לִישָׁן, וְכַד אֲנָא אָמַר לָךְ צֵדוּ בִּישָׁא אַתְּ זְבַן לִי לִישָׁן? א"ל: מִינֵּה טָבְתָא וּמִינֵּה בִּישְׁתָּא־כַּד הֲוָה טָב לֵית טָב מִינֵּיה, וְכַד בִּישׁ לֵית בִּישׁ מִינֵּיה.

Background of the Tale

This midrashic tale deals with the power of the tongue, which can be used for good as well as for evil. There are numerous allusions to the power of the tongue in the Bible and its potential damaging effects. For instance, Proverbs 26:28 says that "a lying tongue hates those who are afflicted by it, while a flattering mouth works ruin." What makes this tale interesting is the fact that the servant of a rabbi is sent to the test, having been asked to find both the best and the worst thing to eat. In both instances the servant returns with a tongue, pointing to its dual nature of being able to formulate words that can be used for beneficial purposes, as well as words that can damage, hurt, and injure.

Speech and Language: What Does Judaism Say?

Normally when one thinks of ethics, one contemplates a person's actions toward another and whether those actions are right or wrong. In Judaism, ethical issues include the ways in which people are to communicate with one another using words in speech. Words can be powerful objects. When used properly, they can soothe, comfort, and bless. When used improperly, they can hurt. In biblical times the power of words had been proclaimed in this well-known warning: "Death and life are in the power of the tongue" (Proverbs 18:21).

There are many rules and laws in Judaism regarding speech and the primary role it plays in our lives. A Jew is forbidden to insult, shame, embarrass, defame, slander, curse, or swear falsely. The nineteenth-century rabbi Israel Meir Hakohen Kagan wrote a book outlining the seriousness of the sin of gossip. In accordance with an old custom, he is often referred to by the book's title, *Chafetz Chayim*, which was drawn from the biblical verse "Who is the person who desires life, loves days, that he may see good therein? Then keep your tongue from evil, and your lips from speaking guile" (Psalm 34:13–14).

In the late nineteenth century, the French Jewish soldier Alfred Dreyfus was falsely accused of having sold secret documents in Germany. In 1894 he was condemned to life imprisonment, the verdict being influenced by invalid documents containing false words that had not been communicated to the defense. Although eventually exonerated and freed, Dreyfus surely realized that it was the power of words that caused his imprisonment.

Words are so commonplace that we often do not stop to think about them and the way in which they ought to be used. Taking them for granted, we often value their power less than we should.

What can words do that is unethical? The power of a person to do harm through communication is so great that it even appears as one of the Ten Commandments. The ninth commandment states: "You shall not bear false witness against your neighbor." That is to say, when giving testimony against a neighbor, be extremely cautious in giving such testimony. Even if the greatest saint and scholar told you that your neighbor had committed a crime, you should not testify unless you yourself actually witnessed the crime.

The ancient Rabbis were deeply aware of the power of speech and communication. The misuse of words includes the use of profanity and foul language as well as talebearing and gossiping about a person. Wanting to make the people aware of it as well, they wrote many stories and were quoted numerous times concerning their attitude on the use of language.

Maimonides defined slander of the tongue as speaking disparagingly about anyone (even though what is spoken may be the truth!). The Sages equated the use of the evil tongue with idolatry, incest, and even murder. It is doubtful whether the Rabbis meant this equation to be taken literally. It was, however, their way of demonstrating their hope that people would avoid committing the crime of slander and gossip by equating it with three of the gravest sins. It is noteworthy that of all transgressions, evil talk is perhaps the one that is easiest to commit, but its effects can be potent enough to destroy a person's reputation.

Notable Quotations

1. Whoever dirties his mouth by speech, even though it had been decreed in heaven that he should live seventy years, causes the decree to be reversed. (Babylonian Talmud, *K'tubot* 8b)

2. Rabbi Yishmael said: "Do not go about as a gossipmonger among your people" [Leviticus 19:16]. Such gossipmongering is the same as *l'shon hara* [slander]. (Jerusalem Talmud, *Pei-ah* 2:1)

3. The person who utters foul language commits a great transgression and becomes despised in the eyes of others, for that person has abandoned the traits of decency and modesty, which are the distinguishing marks of his people, and walks the path of insolent and defiant persons. (*M'norat HaMaor,* chapter on *l'shon hara*)

4. Hot coals, which are cooled on the outside, grow cool within, but gossip and slander, even if cooled outwardly, do not cool inwardly. (Jerusalem Talmud, *Pei-ah* 1:1)

5. The person who slanders, who listens to slander, and who testifies falsely deserves to be thrown to the dogs. (Babylonian Talmud, *P'sachim* 118a)

6. God accepts the repentance of all sins, except the sin of imposing a bad name upon a person slandered. (Babylonian Talmud, *Arachin* 15b)

7. Rabbi Yochanan quoted a teaching of Rabbi Shimon ben Yochai that injurious words constitute a greater wrong than monetary injury. The former affects a man's person, the other his profit. Financial harm can be repaired; personal harm cannot. (Babylonian Talmud, *Bava M'tzia* 58b)

8. One who guards one's tongue and lips is worthy to be clothed with the spirit of holiness. (*Zohar* 4:183b)

9. The person who is vulgar of speech descends to the deepest region of the netherworld. (Babylonian Talmud, *Shabbat* 33a)

10. Even as it is a person's duty to speak what is acceptable, so it is his duty to refrain from speaking what is unacceptable. (Babylonian Talmud, *Y'vamot* 65b)

11. God says of the one who utters slander: "Both of us cannot inhabit the world at the same time." (Babylonian Talmud, *Arachin* 15b)

12. Frustrate the hopes of those who slander us. (Weekday *Amidah* prayer)

13. If one hears something unseemly, one should put one's hands in one's ears. (Babylonian Talmud, *K'tubot* 5a–b)

Questions

1. The Rabbis have remarked that a slanderer's crime is worse than that of a murderer. Can you think of examples? Do you agree or disagree? Explain why.

2. Today, numerous recording groups use obscenities in their lyrics. How do you feel about this? Why? Would you want your own children to listen to such music? Do you think there is any potential conflict between the American value of freedom and the Jewish value of guarding one's tongue? Why or why not? If so, how might you resolve the conflict?

3. The *Amidah* prayer ends with a prayer called *Elohai N'tzor,* asking God to guard my mouth from evil and my lips from speaking falsehood. Do you think that this is a good choice of prayer for the conclusion of the *Amidah?* Why or why not?

4. Research the *Al Cheit* confessional prayer that we recite on Yom Kippur. How many of the transgressions listed in this prayer deal with the use or misuse of language? List all of them if you can.

5. It has been said that people often find a kind of perverse joy in dwelling on and speaking about the faults of others. Why do you think this is so?

6. It has been said that in addition to the prohibition against talebearing, other Torah commandments are violated when a person gossips:

   a. "You shall not place a stumbling block before a blind person" (Leviticus 19:14).
   b. "You shall not hate your brother in your heart" (Leviticus 19:17).

How does gossip serve to violate these two biblical prohibitions?

7. Anger can often lead to inappropriate speech. In a talmudic tale, Elijah the prophet appears to one of the Rabbis to tell him: "Never get drunk and you will not sin. Never lose your temper and you will not sin." Do you agree with this statement? Why or why not? What are some ways that one can work to control one's temper?

8. In order to refrain from gossiping, Dennis Prager and Joseph Telushkin (*Eight Questions People Ask about Judaism,* pg. 175) present some suggestions:

   a. Eliminating gossip at the Friday night Shabbat table.
   b. Avoiding spending time with others who constantly gossip.
   c. Changing the topic with people who gossip.
   d. Not revealing private conversations that you have with others.

What do you think about these suggestions? What others might you have to suggest?

9. A Chasidic saying states that "human beings are God's language." Explain what is meant by this statement.

10. Read the following Chasidic tale.

A man would often slander his rabbi, until one day, feeling remorseful, he begged the rabbi for forgiveness and indicated that he was willing to undergo any penance to make amends. The rabbi told him to take several feather pillows from his home, cut them open and scatter the feathers to the winds. The man did so immediately, and returned to the rabbi to notify him that he had fulfilled his request.

The rabbi then told him, "Go and gather all the feathers that the wind has scattered. For though you are sincerely remorseful and truly desirous of correcting the evil that you have done, it is about as possible to repair the damage done by your words as it will be to recover the feathers."

Can you think of a time when someone did some damage to another through the use of words? Is it possible to teach a person who constantly gossips about others not to do so?

Glossary of Texts and People

Sourcebooks

Avot D'Rabbi Natan: Small talmudic tractate expanding upon the tractate called *Pirkei Avot* (Ethics of the Fathers). It was written by Rabbi Natan the Babylonian.

Babylonian Talmud: The first sourcebook for Jewish law. It is composed of the Mishnah, a six-volume work edited by Y'hudah HaNasi around 200 C.E., and the Gemara, which explains the Mishnah, completed in approximately 500 C.E.

Derech Eretz Rabbah: A small tractate at the end of the Mishnah order *N'zikin*, dealing with laws of personal status, moral sayings, and so on.

Derech Eretz Zuta: A small tractate at the end of the Mishnah order *N'zikin*, containing moral sayings.

Jerusalem Talmud: Compilation of the laws and discussion of the teachers in Israel, mainly in the academy of Tiberias. Much smaller in length than the Babylonian Talmud and considered less authoritative, it was completed sometime at the beginning of the fifth century C.E.

Midrash: Refers to the nonlegal sections of the Talmud and the rabbinic books containing biblical interpretations in the spirit of legends.

Midrash Tanchuma: Attributed to Rabbi Tanchuma bar Aba, the discourses center around the opening verse of the portion of the Bible designated for each week.

Mishneh Torah: The code of law and ethics written by Moses ben Maimon (Maimonides) in the late twelfth century.

M'norat HaMaor: Meaning "Lamp of Illumination," this ethical work was written by Rabbi Israel al-Nakawa of fourteenth-century Spain.

P'sikta D'Rav Kahana: Collection of midrashic homilies from the seventh century C.E.

P'sikta Rabbati: Midrashic collection containing discourses for the Jewish Festivals and special Sabbaths. It was edited in 1880 by Meir Friedman.

Sefer Chasidim: Ethical work by the twelfth-century sage Rabbi Y'hudah HeChasid. It addresses the concerns of everyday life.

Shulchan Aruch: This law code by Rabbi Joseph Karo (1488–1575) serves as a practical guide in the observance of traditional Judaism throughout the world.

Sifra: Oldest rabbinic commentary on the Book of Leviticus.

Yalkut Shimoni: The most comprehensive midrashic collection, this work has been attributed to the thirteenth-century rabbi Simeon of Frankfort.

Zohar: A mystical commentary on the Five Books of Moses.

Persons Quoted

Baal Shem Tov (1700–1760): Israel ben Eliezer, founder of the Chasidic movement.

Buber, Martin (1878–1965): Religious existentialist and philosopher.

Maimonides (1135–1204): Moses ben Maimon. He wrote many important works, include *A Guide for the Perplexed* and a massive fourteen-book code called the *Mishneh Torah*.

Nachman of Bratzlav (1770–1811): A leading Chasidic rabbi, founder of the Bratzlaver Chasidim. He was the grandson of the Baal Shem Tov, founder of the Chasidic movement.

Philo Judaeus (20 B.C.E.–50 C.E.): Philosopher whose Greek writings primarily focused on the Torah.

Rashi (1040–1105): French Bible and Talmud commentator par excellence.

Salanter, Rabbi Israel (1810–1883): Israel ben Ze'ev Wolf, the founder of the so-called Musar or ethical movement.